MW01484261

SUCH STUFF AS STARS ARE MADE OF

*Thoughts on Savoring the Wonders
in Everyday Life*

Wishing you wonder,
Caroline Castle Hicks
2019

SUCH STUFF AS STARS ARE MADE OF

*Thoughts on Savoring the Wonders
in Everyday Life*

CAROLINE CASTLE HICKS

Copyright © 2018, 2007 by Caroline Castle Hicks

All rights reserved. With the exception of short quotations for articles and reviews, no part of this publication may be reproduced, transmitted, scanned, distributed, stored in any form or by any means, electronic, mechanical, photocopying, recording, or otherwise, without prior written permission from the author.

Cover art by Debbie Littledeer.
See more of her work at www.debbielittledeer.com.
Cover design by Susan Alford.
Book design by Maureen Ryan Griffin.
Author photograph by Studio L'Amoreaux

Published in the United States of America by

FLOATING LEAF PRESS

A division of
WordPlay
Maureen Ryan Griffin
6420 A-1 Rea Road, Suite 218,
Charlotte, NC 28277
Email: info@wordplaynow.com
www.wordplaynow.com

Rev. Ed: *Such Stuff As Stars Are Made Of.*

ISBN 978-0-9802304-5-1

To Maureen, incomparable teacher
and phenomenal friend,
and to my mother Wilma,
my sister Claire,
and my daughter Mariclaire—
four strong, wondrous women
who have taught me
to not only gaze at the stars,
but to reach for them.

CONTENTS

INTRODUCTION

According to my mother, I've loved playing with words for even longer than I can remember. She still tells the story of when I was two and received a toy crocodile dressed in a spiffy suit and a straw hat studded with flowers. I held it up for everyone to see and said, "Look! A croco-doll!!" I then succumbed to a fit of two-year-old hilarity at my own joke. Although I have no recollection of this charming toddler moment, it is nonetheless very real for me. Such is the power of words and storytelling to preserve a family's history, to capture moments large and small so that they can be handed down, written down, remembered.

I do recall being five and concocting a secret language with my best friend Marjorie. It was a highly flexible language given that we changed the meaning of most of the words to suit the purpose at hand. We had one inviolate expression, however. *Purlou ongjay*, from the beginning, meant "I love you."

Words are still a source of joy and playfulness for me, but more than that, they are my saving grace. Even as a child, I felt that time passed too quickly, that the good stuff ended long before I was ready to let it go. Back then, it was birthday parties, bedtime stories, trick-or-treating, and Christmas morning that seemed to accelerate beyond my grasp. Now, firmly entrenched in middle age, I find that it is life itself that hurtles by at warp speed. Writing things down as they happen is not only an act of preservation, but a form of salvation, an antidote and a balm to that poignant, almost breathless feeling that life is all too transitory and that nothing lasts.

Writing lasts. Stories last. And they don't have to be the big stories. Interspersed among the ponderous milestones of life are all those tiny crystalline moments worthy of their own legacy. Whether it's the subtle bronzed richness of a November afternoon, a stunning dinner table insight offered by a teenager who is wise beyond her years, or an unexpected gift that proves someone was paying attention after all, our stories are there for the taking every day. Too often we miss them, distracted as we are by the next hurdle, the next big thing. Yet they happen regardless of whether we still need to lose ten pounds, get the kids through college, or clean out the garage. And they are there to be savored—and saved—before they get away.

That is why I write, I think—to counteract the yearning that is so integral to the human condition, to break free from that limbo state that suspends me between a longed-for past and a wished-for future. On any given day, amidst life's frustrations, its tedium, and even its grief, countless wonders spool out before me. By noticing them and sharing them in words, I stake my claim to now.

J. M. Barrie, the author of *Peter Pan*, once wrote: "You must have been warned against letting the golden hours slip by." There is no doubt that our golden hours streak into memory like shooting stars. In the end, of course, it is all memory. But won't the wonders that reside there at the end of the day glow all the more brilliantly for having been savored while they were lived?

BEFORE THE BEGINNING

I was going to say that I like beginnings, but no, let me go back and start again because it's the very beginning of things that I love, and really, that's not even it. No, it's that tiny sparking jewel of time that happens just before something starts. It's the racehorse, poised at the starting gate, ears pricked for the signal that lets him fly. It's the Olympic diver, high above the crowd, bouncing on the balls of her feet, testing the board. It's the symphony conductor, stepping onto the podium, raising his baton, and pausing—just for a second—but in that small silence, all the music hangs there, shimmering.

It's the moment right before the curtain goes up, when the ballerinas wait in the dark, flexing their ankles in their toe shoes, already dancing in their heads—perfectly—with no forgotten steps. It's that inhalation before the candles are blown out, before the song, before the kiss. It's just before the sun rises, the wave breaks, the baby is born.

It is that instant of pure possibility, untouched by failure or loss. Too soon, it will be swallowed up in the after of what is, but how I love that slender cusp of before because it's so full of what might be.

A LONGING WE CAN'T NAME

FALSE SPRING

I open my window to this odd
January breeze, hoping it will stir me,
help the words come. Instead, I sit
drawing in the margins of my notes,
daisies and stick men, unnerved
by a warm wind that bears
only the scent of musty leaves.

My uncle is a peach farmer
north of Greenville. He'd say
it's no good, this weather.
You need the 'chilling hours';
the trees need time to rest.

I told him once the winter orchard
made me sad. Walking on a day like this,

among his trees, I saw only acres
of bare limbs, pruned and supplicant.

The peaches are always there,
he said, stopping now and then to check
a random branch. He nicked them
with his pocketknife, hoping
for no sign of buds, yet showing me
the green within.

We walked the whole farm wordless
then, his dogs nosing old pits
in the brittle grass, chasing
drowsy foxes, warmed from their dens.

I still can't help longing
for the April orchard,
white and glorious, heady
with the drone of bees.
Or the summer orchard, laden,
branches brought low.

But it's easier when I remember
that even now, the fruit is there,
hidden and silent,
gathering itself.

FEBRUARY

"How do you spell *violence*?"
my daughter calls from the kitchen,
her words swallowed by walls
and the turn of the stairwell.

She is eight and I wonder,
as I call back letter by letter,
what she wants with such a word.

She appears in the doorway
of my room where I fold
a pile of laundry on the bed,
trying to match the baby's socks.
"Violets has an *n*?" she asks.
"It must be silent."

She is making Valentines,
sweet simple ones with doilies,
cut-out hearts and roses-are-red.

She looks down at the scissors
in her hand, wanting me to notice
how she holds them by the sharp end,
the way I taught her.

In her other hand is
a crooked red heart with lace edges
and I am sure she's left
a trail of paper bits
coming up the stairs
like Gretl with her breadcrumbs.

She walks to my window, looking
beyond the feeble lamplight at my bed.
Outside the afternoon is muffled in gray;
the dead grass and damp sidewalks
are the color of mushrooms.
"It'll snow tonight," she says.

I won't tell her it's too warm for snow,
that there may be cold rain for days.

She is too happy believing
in possibilities.

And who am I to argue
about a matter of degrees?
When just a shift of wind could
blow a blizzard in, or make
the winter sun return
to try and coax
a crocus from the ground.

A PLACE BY THE SEA

My family has a little place on Topsail Island, near Wilmington, North Carolina. We rent it out mostly, in order to pay for it, and we go there when we can. Over the past several years, hurricanes have hit Topsail hard, destroying dozens of houses and damaging dozens more. In their wake, they left dunes where the road used to be and took big chunks of the island with them. Even so, things could have been far worse. Topsail, like all of North Carolina's barrier islands, is but a slender finger of sand, anchored by little more than scrub pines and sea oats, more akin to the water than to the land. If the winds had been stronger, the storm surge higher, Topsail itself might have washed out to sea.

Though we hate to admit it, our hold on these islands is both tenuous and temporary. Over time, in bites big and small, the ocean will probably reclaim all of them, from Corolla down to Bald Head, taking along with them all the T-shirt shops, the fishing piers, and the beach houses with their cedar siding and their names like *Pelican's Roost* and *Cares Aweigh*.

So far, we've been lucky. Our condo, part of a newer development in Surf City, has survived intact. But what about next time? And the next? All summer long, I watch the nightly weather report with a wary eye and ask myself some hard questions about why we humans carry on this dangerous love affair with beach property. Though even the Bible admonishes us not to build our houses on the sand, we do it anyway, staking claim after claim on highly uncertain ground. And when the winds and floods come, as they always do, we shake our heads in dismay at the resulting devastation. Then, as if resetting so many bowling pins, we go out as soon as the skies have cleared and put everything back up again.

The sea has always made us foolish. Drawn to her rhythm and mystery, we simply cannot stay away. Indeed, because we are such contrary creatures, the danger may be the very thing that compels us to confront the ocean on her own terms. She certainly has no regard for ours.

Yet when we stand at the water's edge, our toes gripping the wet sand that shifts constantly beneath us, the surf pounding in our ears like our own hearts beating, we know there is something beyond the danger, something eternal that even the least introspective among us cannot fail to recognize. Eons ago, we came from here. It feels like home.

Somewhere out to sea, there is always a maelstrom brewing. But as long as the moon tugs at the tides, the ocean will tug at us and we will go, because between the storms, her gifts are so great. We will go for those long walks on the beach at night when a full moon cuts a swath of light across water so still that the waves only whisper at our feet. We will go for those windows left open to the sea air, where the muslin curtains flutter over shells scattered on the sill and the surf lulls us to sleep. And we will go for those golden summer days when the sea sends forth her gentle, frothy fingers to tickle our babies' toes. We will go because that place where earth and water meet is magic, and for so many of us, fulfills a longing we cannot even name.

MAUI MORNING

It is early morning on our first day in Maui.
The first thing I notice as I step out of the condo
onto the lanai is the air, air that has traveled over
thousands of miles of open ocean, air so pure and
sweet it makes me giddy. Air that smells like
flowers, as heady as champagne. Then there is
the light, artist's light, angled and golden, gliding
down the emerald slopes of Haleakala, the sacred
volcano the great god Maui named *The House of
the Sun*. It is there, high above us, far above the
terraced pineapple fields, that the eastern lip of
the ancient crater embraces the island's first light
each day. Then down, down the light comes until
it washes over us and out into the sea. On this
morning, the trade winds are calm and the water
in the sheltered bay is mirror-smooth. Training
our gaze beyond the shoreline, we seek out what

we came here for, the telltale puffs of vapor, the exhalations of whales. They greet us almost immediately, spout after spout, along with fin slaps and fluke-up dives, and sometimes, when we are lucky, with full breaches, fifty-ton creatures jumping for joy. Mostly though, it is the pieces of whales we see, hinting at something wondrous just below the surface. They allow us only glimpses, but it is enough. Some things are meant to be a mystery.

We eat breakfast outside this morning as we will all week long, our binoculars sharing space with the silverware on the table. There are warm macadamia muffins from the bakery nearby which we spread with sweet butter and poha berry jam. There is fresh pineapple whose fragrance fills the air before we even cut it. And there is Kona Gold, the rich, mellow coffee grown on the neighboring Big Island, coffee so delicious and so rare, it has the taste of something illicit.

We will have only seven mornings in Paradise and we will spend each one of them here. Letting go of our ingrained need for agendas and itineraries, we will allow ourselves to simply be. After a few precious trips to Maui,

I have come to realize that I am different here. Me, whose idea of daring is a pair of skinny jeans. Only on Maui can I wear a pareo, that uninhibited tropical garment that is nothing more than a sheet, knotted in strategic places. On Maui, I go barefoot all day, eat mangoes out of my hand, and wear orchids in my hair.

No, seven mornings is not enough time to spend in this place I love most in the world. But fortunately, when I am lucky enough to be here, I have learned how to be still, learned how to let Maui settle into my soul for safekeeping.

And so, on this first morning, I sit back in the cushioned rattan rocker on the open lanai, a steaming mug of Kona in my hands. I watch the golden morning light drift down the mountainside, stirring the birds into song in the flaming poinciana trees. Exulting in the warm caress of gentle, scented trade winds, I breathe deeply of plumeria, torch ginger, and salt spray, while out on the horizon, the baby whales play in a glassy, sapphire sea.

GRANDDAUGHTER PEACHES

All summer long, my next-door neighbor has the rather unsettling habit of showing up at my back door unannounced. A retired Army officer in his seventies, he still carries himself with the precise steps and erect posture of the soldier he once was, knocking at the door with brisk, resounding taps as if for roll call. Since he and his wife moved in several years ago, I have learned never to come downstairs in my nightgown after eight a.m. for fear of finding this spry elderly gentleman peering through the glass door with one hand over his eyes and the other holding a bulging bag of homegrown produce.

Having grown up on a farm in South Carolina, he has made a valiant attempt to return to his roots by transforming his sloping suburban backyard into a miniature and somewhat haphazard facsimile of a peach orchard. His lawn is dotted with a vast variety of peach trees in various stages of growth, but there is not much evidence of a master plan. I must confess that it has become a guilty, voyeuristic pleasure to observe from my kitchen window the almost comical exasperation of his weekly lawn service as they attempt to weave their riding mowers among the trees. I have no doubt they charge him extra for the aggravation. Nevertheless, my neighbor remains undeterred, continuing to insert saplings into the ground at a steady pace, despite the fact that a number of his more mature trees are now producing a truly frightening amount of fruit.

Now don't get me wrong; I adore peaches. A fresh-picked peach, heavy with juice and warmed by the sun, is one of the sublime pleasures of life and I am humbly grateful for this dear man's generosity. But there are only so many peaches that one can peel, eat, freeze, or re-gift to friends, and only so much peach crisp, peach pie, and peach cobbler that one can prepare and consume over the course of a single summer. So it was with growing trepidation that I continued to answer the familiar rap at my door as the sultry days of last August moved languidly toward September, and this would-be farmer's beloved trees grew ever more laden with their swan song of abundance.

By Labor Day weekend, my family and I had reached such a level of peach surfeit that I knew I would have to employ a method of refusal far more assertive than the polite, euphemistic—yet so often ineffective—subtlety that we Southerners are known for. It was not long after coming to this resolution that I answered my door with what was probably a thinly veiled look of horror to find him holding not one, but two, overflowing plastic grocery bags full of small white peaches the size of apricots. At that point, I am sad to say, all feelings of gratitude had been sublimated by one overriding thought along the lines of "Oh, dear God, no."

It was then, too, though, that I knew I would take them yet again. There was something in his face this time, a mixture of pride, love—wistfulness?—that told me there was something different about these peaches. Not that it mattered. I realized in a moment of surrender that I was never going to refuse this old warrior's offerings. It just wasn't in me.

"I hope you can use these," he said, handing me the bags which were accompanied by twin swarms of fruit flies. "They're a little different, not quite as sweet—might take some getting used to, but I think you'll like them. They have kind of a perfume. Can you smell it?"

I could. It was heady, musky, almost exotic.

"Oh, and watch out for the worms. These tend to have more worms than usual. But just cut them out and you'll be fine."

"As long as I don't find half a worm," I replied with Meryl Streep-worthy cheer, feeling the bile rise at the back of my throat and contemplating the hour or two I would spend peeling small, crawling peaches that would "take some getting used to."

"Well, enjoy;" he said, turning to go down the back steps, "these are probably the last."

Then, before I could formulate some suitably regretful reply to this parting remark, he paused and turned back, looking more wistful than ever. "You know, I meant to tell you that these are kind of special. I've always loved peaches—I guess you can tell that—and whenever I got a day of leave in Vietnam, I'd try to get to the village market to see if they had any. I found

these there and I liked them so much that I saved
a few of the pits and brought them home to plant
on the family farm in South Carolina. They did
real well and I've kept trees growing from those
pits ever since." Smiling, he pointed at the bags I
still held in my hands. "So I guess you could say
you've got some granddaughter peaches there."

I looked down at the bags and back up at
him. "Wow," I said, and it came out on a sigh.
"Thank you."

Already walking away, he waved with a sort
of salute. "You let me know how you like those.
I eat them for breakfast with milk and sugar."

I thought about a lot of things that night as,
swathed in juice and fruit flies and a smell like
hothouse flowers, I washed and peeled all those
peaches, creating the space in my busy life for a
chore that had somehow become a sacred act.
But mostly, I thought of the way that beauty
always rights itself. Always. It might be in the
delicate, yet tenacious way that wild raspberries
were said to have tangled themselves in the
barbed wire of Auschwitz. It might be in the
bold, defiant way the sunset must have seared the
Pacific sky on the evening after Pearl Harbor. Or
it might be in the unexpected, slow-in-coming

way of a few dried peach pits carried home in the pocket of a war-weary soldier and planted on a boyhood farm. In the generations of trees, fragrant with springs of white blossoms and heavy with summer upon summer of fruit to be given away.

A SEASON IN-BETWEEN

It is the Thursday after Labor Day, no longer summer, not yet fall. At loose ends, I sit down to breakfast. It has rained all week, the sodden remnants of a hurricane. But this morning is scrubbed and brilliant, the first sun in days tumbling across the table, across the last of the peaches I have sliced onto a chipped plate. I eat them slowly—how could I not?—when they remind me of winter and their absence.

I watch the hummingbirds fight over the feeder just outside the window, fueling up on nectar for the journey ahead. By the back door, my last three tomatoes redden, in defiance of their waterlogged pot and spent vine.

It is the crickets I hear now, not the cicadas. The spiders grow busy; webs sparkle under the eaves. There is a restlessness to the trees, even on this lustrous morning, as if they are anxious to get on with things.

I suppose I should feel wistful, should feel, perhaps, even a touch of despair, yet how can I?—when even the days of a fading season come drenched as they are with the Divine.

LESSONS FROM THE NIGHT SKY

There are times, usually on clear winter nights, when I can still see a sky full of stars from my driveway in Huntersville, North Carolina. There is never the profound darkness or the endless sparkling canopy that I have been privileged to witness high in the Rocky Mountains or from the empty dunes near Ocracoke on the Outer Banks, but I welcome any chance to look into the night sky and find the universe winking back at me.

I've read a lot in recent years about the increasing amount of light pollution in urban areas, about how the stars our ancestors steered their lives by have become harder and harder to see. This is troubling because, with apologies to Shakespeare, we are not only "such stuff as dreams are made of." We are such stuff as stars are made of, too, and as incongruous as it may sound, when we can no longer seek out Orion or the North Star or the Milky Way, we will have, in essence, lost touch with our roots.

This was brought home to me in one of those lifechanging ways, when in November of 2001, the Leonid meteor shower put on a show the likes of which had not been seen in thirty years. My husband and I set our alarm for four a.m. and woke to a spectacular display taking place beyond our east-facing windows. As it turned out, the best vantage point was from the picture window above the big tub in our bathroom. We huddled there in our bathrobes and watched in awe as countless meteors streaked across the sky.

We didn't want our space-loving seven-year-old to miss this, but hesitated waking him since the result is often similar to poking a wasp nest with a stick. Taking the indirect approach, we began talking—loudly—and sure enough, he wandered in a short time later, only mildly irritated. "Cool!" he said as he peered out the window with us, his eyes widening in amazement. We watched together for a few minutes and when my husband vacated his spot in the tub in favor of a warm bed, our son grabbed his blanket and climbed in beside me, questions tumbling forth as rapidly as the falling stars outside.

Will they fall on the house, he wanted to know. *Are they made of fire or ice? Where do they come from? Where do they go? How do they stop?*

They were, I realized, some of the elemental questions of life, and though I didn't have all the answers, he didn't seem to mind. He just kept watching and after a while, the questions stopped. I reached out to put my arm around him and he snuggled against my shoulder, something he'd begun doing less and less lately, something I had begun to miss.

We have done our best to illuminate our planet. We have put light everywhere and in doing so, have often blinded ourselves to the beauty of the unknown. But as long as there are human beings hurtling through space on this little green sphere, we will need dark places and open skies. We will need them to make us feel small, yet utterly connected to the infinite. We will always need them, so that we can hold our children close—and look up—hoping to see the stars dance.

LET NOVEMBER COME FIRST

When I was a child, Halloween was the smell of burnt pumpkin, the taste of cheap chocolate, and the feel of a plastic mask that made my face sweat. It was a glorious, sugar-fix free-for-all that was an entity unto itself. There was no point in thinking about Christmas yet, since it was still light years away.

Now when I blow out the flaming pool of wax in the family jack-o'-lantern on Halloween night, I still breathe in that deeply reminiscent smell. But as I stand there in the darkness, I feel a poignant sense of loss and a quickening anxiety. The winds have picked up; the Holiday Vortex has begun.

Not that the signs weren't already there. Christmas decorations started appearing in stores in late September, close on the heels of the

Halloween decorations which materialized by Labor Day, and not long after the back-to-school displays which showed up right after the Fourth of July. It's as though we are speeding through life in fast-forward, racing toward milestones large and small. By the time each one arrives, however, it's become an anticlimax because we are already projecting ourselves toward the next one.

At no time is this more apparent than in November, a month that has suffered an identity crisis for years. What has November become, anyway, but an extra four weeks that we forward-thinking people use to make December manageable?

I love Christmas; I always have. Just not yet. All the catalogues and mall decorations and the "last-minute-shopping" ads screaming at me before Thanksgiving are like eating too many pretzels before dinner. By the time the real food is ready, I'm not even hungry.

So I say, let's take back November. Yes, the glory days of autumn are over. The leaves have fallen; the kids have colds; the gray days increase. And whirling ahead is the great Vortex, just waiting to suck us in. No matter. For a few days, let's hide the catalogues and stay away from the mall. Let's find a way to celebrate November. She has her own gentle secrets to share.

When it's sunny in November, the light is beautiful. In the late afternoon, it falls low and golden, burnishing the landscape. When you get out of your car to grab the dry cleaning or run into the post office, stop for a minute and turn your face toward the sun. Let the breeze lift your hair. Take a few deep breaths.

On a dismal November weekend (and there always is one), bake some bread or make some soup. Wear fuzzy socks and play board games. Light a fire, sit back, and pretend you can remember what it was like to have nothing to do.

Find a pond or a lake on some mist-shrouded morning and watch for geese. Geese belong to November. Bring a blanket and a thermos of something hot. Find a rock to sit on and wait for them. Before long, they will descend in perfect V-formation onto the still water, their melancholy honking punctuating the silence. Feel the warm mug in your hands, the dampness on your cheeks.

While you're at it, take a walk in the November woods, preferably the morning after a soaking rain. If you're lucky, it will be a perfect Indian Summer day with brilliant turquoise skies streaked with the brushstrokes of cirrus clouds. Remember the way it felt when your face and hands were cold, but you still wanted to take off your sweater and tie it around your waist? Hold out for a day like that. The leaves have not yet blackened, but lie at your feet in a matted carpet of red and gold and brown. Here in North Carolina, the smell of the November woods is intoxicating, a heady mixture of pine, butternut, and all those other fresh forest smells you wish you could identify. With the canopy gone, the woods are open, allowing you to see the stunning architecture of trees.

November is by nature an introspective month. It's a good place to put Thanksgiving, a good time for cultivating gratitude. This year, perhaps we can make Thanksgiving weekend more than just the starting gun for the final Yuletide sprint. For most of my adult life, I have longed to enter December without a sense of overwhelming urgency, to experience the season of Advent as it was intended, as a time of hushed, yet joyful expectation. A time of waiting. Christmas will be here soon enough and will pass just as quickly as any November Monday. The trick is in giving both their due.

So let me have November with its damp, chill evenings, its barren trees, its clear fall light. Let's take back November and just maybe, we'll get back Christmas, too.

KEEPING CHRISTMAS

The year our Christmas tree fell, our son Ian was still a baby, and in our sleep-deprived state, my husband and I had forgotten the time-honored safeguard of securing the tree to the staircase banister with a length of nylon fishing line. Consequently, we were awakened one night a couple of weeks before Christmas, not by reindeer hooves on the roof, but by an unmistakable whooshing thump, accompanied by the muffled sound of tinkling glass, ominous in its delicacy.

I've always loved the holiday season and like the reformed Scrooge in *A Christmas Carol*, strive to "keep Christmas well." So for me, this was a catastrophe of operatic proportions. I will never forget rushing down the darkened stairs, flipping on a light switch, and finding our lush

Fraser fir passed out on the floor in a tangle of light strings and the shattered remains of a treasured ornament collection spanning several generations of my family's history. It was all I could do not to be sick right there on the spot.

The next morning, after surveying the destruction in the light of day and salvaging what little I could, I called the first person who came to mind, our adopted Tante Helga, my family's beloved German "auntie," who started off as our daughter's kindergarten teacher and ended up becoming as close to us as anyone bound by blood. I'm not sure how it happened, but there was a connection between us from the very beginning, as if we were long-lost relatives who had finally been reunited. Who knows? Perhaps there was a link somewhere in our shared German ancestry that caused a flash of recognition when our paths finally crossed.

Helga and I quickly discovered that, despite our age difference, we were kindred spirits in countless ways, but especially in our love of German Christmas traditions. Although well into her sixties by the time we met, she had lost none of her childlike enthusiasm for the magic, as she called it—the old European carols, the buttery cookies, the real fir tree adorned with cherished blown glass ornaments. Having gifted two generations of lucky five-year-olds with her almost mythic brand of Christmas spirit, she was sure to understand, better than anyone, the depth of my dismay.

Sure enough, she responded as I knew she would, with a typical outpouring of love and *mitleid*, that wonderful German word for pity, compassion, and empathy all rolled into one. "Oh, my dear Caroline," I recall her saying in her heavily accented English, "it is heartbreaking to lose things that are so precious. Every year, when you take the ornaments out of the box, you unwrap so many memories. It feels as though you are holding your childhood in your hands, doesn't it?" Sounding close to tears, she sighed before continuing.

"You know, I remember coming back to our town after the war, after all the bombing. I wondered what it was that I kept seeing, something sparkling in the trees. And finally, I realized." She paused to take a slow breath. "It was bits of colored glass. Bits of Christmas ornaments that caught in the trees when everyone's attics blew up."

She said this almost matter-of-factly, without a trace of judgment or condescension, as if she was merely commiserating, as if my experience somehow compared to hers. I, on the other hand, was rendered speechless by the contrast. The scene she conjured up in those few words was so vivid in my imagination that I couldn't begin to fathom how she lived with the actual memory. And this was just one of many memories, some most certainly unspeakable, bound up and carried for more than sixty years.

Yet here was a woman who, despite a childhood wiped away by World War II—or perhaps because of it—"kept Christmas" better than anyone I've ever known. Each year, for several decades now, a new set of five-year-olds gathers at her house for a holiday party, complete with a one-woman puppet show and a huge, made-from-scratch gingerbread house with a light to illuminate the tiny gingerbread table and chairs inside. And every year, little faces are awash in delight and little fingers pinch off gum drops and peppermints when no one is looking. "Children don't question the magic," she says, and it is all the reason she needs to work so hard at creating it.

In light of what Helga told me, I might have apologized for making such a big deal out of our tree incident, but there was no need. Her sympathy, her *mitleid*, was genuine. In her hard-won wisdom, Helga knows all too well that being human carries with it the common thread of loss, that it weaves a unique design in every life. Is it fair? Almost never, but by sharing her story of loss with me, she honored mine.

In the end, of course, the toppled tree confirmed what I already knew about Christmas. As soon as the word got out, our loved ones began to shower us with ornaments, some of them even parting with beloved family keepsakes in their effort to make us feel better. Our collection, replenished by grace, is more beautiful than ever now, and while it will never be the same, it has a story and a legacy of its own.

It's true that some of us are a little crazier about Christmas than others, but I've found I can't apologize for that, either. Rather, I feel a kinship with another literary character who predates Scrooge by about three hundred years. It was Cervantes' Don Quixote who believed that "too much sanity may be madness, and maddest of all, to see life as it is and not as it should be." For Helga, for me, and for everyone else who loves the season and the spirit as we do, Christmas, well-kept, is life as it should be.

A TASTE FOR LEMON SORBET

Every year, during that peculiar no-man's-land of time between Christmas and New Year's, I've been known to indulge in a rather unbecoming fit of post-holiday blues. The Christmas season, with its lights and fir trees, its butter cookies and general coziness, has always been my favorite time of year. As an adult, I must confess that I have continued to succumb to that childlike after-Christmas melancholy, when after all those weeks of buildup and anticipation, I must accept the reality that the party is most definitely over. Each year, as I've walked listlessly from room to room, surveying a tree that is dropping an increasing number of needles, a Christmas tablecloth now decorated with bread crumbs and cranberry stains, and tins upon tins of goodies that are tasting staler by the day, I have despaired that there is nothing left but to leave the warmth of candles and carols behind and venture out into the bleak and barren wasteland that is January.

I might have continued this pathetic yearly tradition for the rest of my life if my fourteen-year-old daughter Mariclaire had not chosen to reveal herself as a philosopher—and perhaps, a budding psychologist and poet as well. Upon once again hearing my pitiful lament at having to box up all the decorations and toss our pretty tree on the curb, she cast me one of those fed-up, assessing glances at which teenagers are so adept.

"Mom," she said, "I know I'm supposed to be sad that Christmas is over, but I'm not. I like January. Christmas is great and everything, but it's kind of like eating cheesecake. The first few bites are really good, but then it starts tasting too rich and you just want to push it away and have something like lemon sorbet. To me, January is lemon sorbet."

Now, as a writer, I am always on the lookout for a good metaphor and a mother's bias notwithstanding, I had to admit that this was one of the best I'd heard in quite a while. And like many a memorable and pithy remark, hers had the power to alter a whole way of thinking. Unwittingly, my wise daughter had given me the gift of a fresh perspective and I resolved then and there to quit whining and to begin viewing the entire de-Christmas-ing process in a new light. Rather than seeing it as a depressing chore, just maybe I could turn it into a kind of sacrament, a benediction to the old year and a path-clearing for the new one.

The philosopher Simone Weil once said that "the future is made of the same stuff as the present." To some extent, I think that's true, but in light of my daughter's philosophy, it seems a bit jaded now. In January, if we let it, the future can feel like different stuff. Newer stuff.

As a symbolic gesture, I made some lemon sorbet for the family, and although it's sometimes hard to tell with fourteen-year-olds, I think Mariclaire was pleased at my ability to come around. And as I stood there squeezing lemons in my newly undecorated kitchen, their clean, citrus scent filled the room, infusing the air with freshness and the unmistakable tang of possibility.

WEARING IT WELL

OUT OF MY HANDS

How do you do that, asks my three-year-old son,
make the words come out of your hand?
He stands at my elbow
as I write the grocery list—

> *Apples,* with their short-stemmed *p*'s,
> *Bread,* sturdy, buttressed by *b* and *d,*
> *Milk,* its fluid *m* poured out,
> A box of small, round *eggs.*

How do I explain
that out of fusion and division,
out of cataclysms of bone and blood
and the birth of whole populations of cells,

> comes this,

the movement of pen across paper,
the countless impulses and connections
that create

your wonder,

my surprise,

at the questions you ask
and the way they prove miracles.

SECOND SKIN

My favorite pair of old jeans will never fit me again. I have finally accepted this immutable truth. After nurturing and giving birth to two babies, my body has undergone a metamorphosis. I may have returned to my pre-baby weight, but subtle shifts and expansions have taken place, my own version of continental drift. As a teenager, I never understood the difference between junior and misses sizing; misses clothing just looked old. Now it is all too clear that wasp-waists and micro-fannies are but the fleeting trappings of youth. But that's OK, because while the jeans no longer button, the life I exchanged for them fits better than they ever did.

For me, this is a barefoot, shorts and T-shirt time of life. I have slipped so easily into young motherhood; it is the most comfortable role I have ever worn. No rough seams, no snagging zippers. Just a feeling that I have stepped out of the dressing room in something that finally feels right.

I love the feel of this baby on my hip, his soft head a perfect fit under my chin, his tiny hands splayed out like small pink starfish against my arms. I love the way my eight-year-old daughter walks alongside us as we cross the sunny grocery store parking lot. On gorgeous spring days, the breeze lifts her wispy ponytail and we laugh at how the sunshine makes the baby sniff and squint. I am constantly reaching out to touch them, the way a seamstress would two lengths of perfect silk, envisioning what might be made from them, yet hesitant to alter them, to lose the weight of their wholeness in my hands.

On those rare mornings when I wake up before they do, I go into their rooms and watch them sleeping, their faces creased and rosy. Finally, they squirm and stretch themselves awake, reaching out for a hug. I gather them up, bury my face in them, and breathe deeply. They are like towels just pulled from the dryer, tumbled warm and cottony.

Sometimes I follow the sound of girlish voices to my daughter's room where she and her friends play dress-up, knee-deep in garage sale chiffon, trying life on for size. Fussing and preening in front of the mirror, they drape themselves in cheap beads and adjust tiaras made of sequins and cardboard. I watch these little girls with their lank, shiny hair that no rubber bands or barrettes seem able to tame. They are constantly pushing errant strands behind their ears, and in that grown-up gesture, I see glimpses of the women they will become. I know that too soon these clouds of organdy and lace will settle permanently into their battered boxes, the ones that have served as treasure chests and princess thrones. They will become the hand-me-downs of my daughter's girlhood, handed back to me.

For now, though, my children curl around me on the sofa in the evening, often falling asleep, limbs limp and soft against me like the folds of a well-worn nightgown. For now, we still adorn each other and they are content to be clothed in my embrace. I know there will be times that will wear like scratchy wool sweaters and four-inch heels. We will have to try on new looks together, tugging and scrunching, trying to keep the basic fabric intact. By then, we will have woven a complicated tapestry with its own peculiar pattern, its snags and pulls and tears.

But I will not forget *this* time, of drowsy heads against my shoulder, of footy pajamas and mother-daughter dresses, of small hands clasped in mine. This time fits me. I plan to wear it well.

MY SON, MY SWEET POTATO

When my son Ian was four, that perfect little boy age of winsomeness and innocence, of endless questions, busy fingers, and tiny white baby teeth, he ran to me one morning after preschool, his *Sesame Street* backpack dangling from one slim shoulder. "Look, Mommy, look!!" he yelled, careening down the long church hallway, an obvious treasure clutched in his hands. He held it up to me as he approached, a Styrofoam cup containing a toothpick-impaled sweet potato and about a tablespoon of water, the original cupful having sloshed vigorously over the sides on its way down the hall.

"This is a real sweet potato, Mommy," he said, thrusting it into my hands, "and see, it doesn't look like me at all."

He was, I realized, setting me straight. Although I'd been calling him *Sweet Potato* since he was born, his dawning confusion at being compared to this knobby orange root vegetable was understandable. How was he to know that when it comes to terms of endearment, we Southerners borrow heavily from all kinds of produce and baked goods? *Pumpkin, Honey, Muffin,* and *Sweet Pea* are also on my frequently employed menu of favorites, but the list is endless, requiring only a high sugar content as a common denominator.

I decided to keep things simple. "Well," I said as we walked to the car, "you're much cuter than a sweet potato, that's true, but they are sweet, just like you."

"You mean they taste like cookies?" he asked, more dubious than hopeful.

"Well, maybe not exactly like cookies, but I could fix you one and you could see for yourself."

"But not this one!" he said, looking alarmed. "Our teacher says we have to put this one in the window and grow roots on it. And then we have to stick it in the dirt and it'll make leaves and turn into a plant and make even more sweet potatoes. Can we do that, Mommy?"

"Sure we can," I said, careful to keep my doubts about the outcome of this endeavor to myself. Having no experience in potato farming, but abundant experience in preschool botany experiments, I could only envision a smelly, decaying mess heading from the windowsill to the yard waste bin in a matter of weeks. But then, that was before I knew sweet potatoes.

All winter long, Ian kept vigil over his potato in its place of honor in a sunny kitchen window. Within a month, its root system had taken over the cup and we had to start transferring it every few weeks into larger and larger glass jars. By the time the danger of frost had passed, it was sending up a profusion of heart-shaped, pale green leaves and begging to be planted outside where it belonged. So on a balmy April afternoon, Ian and I headed for the back yard, potting soil and Miracle-Gro in hand.

At this point, I must confess that while I adore the spiritual concept of gardening—that whole lovely idea of drawing sustenance from Mother Earth—the reality has always been a little too earthy for me. There is all that bending and digging and sweating, and then there are the bugs and slugs and dirt. So early on, I found my salvation in container gardening since it's, well, contained, thus providing me with a false but welcome sense of mastery over my environment. Filling an extra-large plastic pot with a mixture of soil and cow manure (which now comes in bags with the smell baked out of it, saints be praised), my little boy and I carefully transferred our fledgling sweet potato vine into its new home on our sunny patio. It then promptly began to grow at a rate similar to those time-elapsed flower-opening sequences on old TV nature shows. By the end of the week, it had doubled in size and by Memorial Day weekend, it had long since escaped the confines of our feeble pot and had sent runners down the sides where they took root in the rock-hard North Carolina clay beyond the concrete slab. I could have cut them back, I know, but by this point, I was overcome by a sort of morbid fascination at the sci-fi element of the whole scenario. Besides, Ian was bursting with pride over his own version of Jack's beanstalk, despite the fact that he seemed to be growing a little afraid of it.

Around the end of June, when we went out one morning to hose down our *Little Shop of Horrors* wannabe and water the more genteel tomato and herb plants, I noticed that the original sweet potato pot was lopsided and figured it was probably just sitting crooked in its drip dish. Shifting the pot a little, I could tell there was something in the way and when I tilted it up to look underneath, I discovered an entire sweet potato growing naked in the dish. "How did my potato get down there?!" Ian asked, his eyes huge, and it took me a minute to assure him that, no, it had not crawled down through the pot, but had sent a root right through the drainage hole and made a brand-new potato, a potato which had grown to large proportions amidst the slugs and roly-polies without the benefit of any soil at all. After that, he refused to water his plant without me close by.

In my ignorance and pessimism, I guess I had never really believed we would grow actual sweet potatoes, but that fall, when the monstrous tangle of vines began to brown and wither, Ian and I went out with our little trowels to poke around and see what else might turn up. It was then that I had to rethink the whole "term of endearment" thing in regard to this particular food source. The three-pound bull taters we pulled out of that overtaxed pot were worthy of their own names. *Hoss* and *Spike* came to mind—and maybe *Bubba*. And when I hacked away the vines to uncover the ground just beyond the patio and started digging there with a full-grown shovel, I unearthed bad boys big enough for a pie apiece with enough brute strength to buckle cement. No, I decided, sweet potato was not something to call an innocent child.

Nevertheless, this tattooed, Harley rider of the vegetable world had earned not only our respect but our loyalty as well, and this fall, Ian and I will harvest the sixth generation of sweet potatoes descended from that original super tuber. This baby of mine who sat in his booster seat cradling his potato on the drive home from preschool is now a strapping ten-year-old, spending hours in the woods building forts with his buddies, racing around on his bike, and zapping aliens on his Xbox. I can still hug him, but only when no one is looking. We are sweet potato experts now, my son and I, but we haven't become jaded. Every October, when we harvest our annual crop together, it's still like finding buried treasure.

Over the years, I've learned that raising boys and potatoes is a messy, unpredictable, and dirt-dependent business, thwarting my efforts to contain either one. My boy and his sweet potatoes have busted the seams of my control, surprising me, often scaring me, but making us all grow. I've learned that sometimes we have to cast off the Styrofoam cup, the outgrown plastic pot, and send out runners, even into hard, resisting ground where, despite the odds, it is altogether possible to thrive. These days, I still call my son *Sweet Potato* when I can get away with it. I've learned it's a pretty good nickname after all.

CLOAKED IN ROMANCE

I went into Stein Mart the other day looking for a pair of khaki pants and a couple of casual shirts, preferably knit, in dark colors, good for hiding jelly stains and crayon marks. Thirty minutes later, I came out of there with a full-length black velvet evening cloak lined in satin with an elaborate brocade clasp at the neck.

I have wanted a black velvet cloak all my life, something to make me feel mysterious and alluring—like Meryl Streep in *The French Lieutenant's Woman*. I want to stand at the end of some long pier, gray clouds scudding overhead, the cape billowing grandly behind me, hair flying in wisps about my face, orchestral music swelling in the background.

In due time, a swarthy English hunk strides up to me wearing knee breeches, black riding boots, and a big-sleeved white shirt (also billowing). He takes me by the shoulders, looks beseechingly into my eyes, and tells me—his deep voice breaking—that he will die without me. At that point, I either remain aloof and enigmatic or I swoon into his arms, depending on my mood. Let's face it; I'm not going to get this fantasy with stain-resistant khakis and a polo shirt.

I often wonder if I wasn't born into the wrong century given my unapologetic passion for all that romantic stuff. I love loads of fabric, lace, and ruffles. I love getting dressed up and feeling elegant. I love courtliness and fancy-pants manners. In truth, however, any century prior to the twentieth would not have suited me very well. The absence of sippy cups, baby wipes, and epidurals would have been a problem. So it's probably best I just pretend.

Pretending doesn't come cheap, though. There's going to be a two-hundred-dollar charge on my Visa this month and I still don't have what I need.

Then again, maybe I do.

STRONG IN THE WAYS OF THE FORCE

*Broadcast on WFAE in May 2005 in
anticipation of the final* Star Wars *movie*

A long time ago in a decade far, far away, I
was enthralled, as most kids were, with the
original episode of *Star Wars*. I was a teenager
when it first came out, and though I'd never been
a fan of science fiction movies, there was
something different about this one. Sure, the
acting was cheesy and Princess Leia's cinnamon-
roll hairdo defined the term *bad hair day*, but
nonetheless, the unfolding saga held all the
elements of epic storytelling. It was a heroic
odyssey played out in interstellar space, full of
dark family secrets, hidden identities, betrayal,
and redemption. And there was the *Force*, with
its mystical yin and yang of darkness and light. I

was hooked from the minute the now-legendary opening words started scrolling up the screen.

Make the jump into hyperspace to 2005 and I've got a young Jedi of my own, a ten-year-old youngling who channels Luke Skywalker and is appalled that he has to go to school on the day the final episode is released. In his mind, it should be a national holiday. This is a child who absorbs *Star Wars* lore and trivia the way a black hole absorbs matter, who can regale you with untold gigabytes of information about droids, Wookiees, and above all, light sabers. "Is there anything cooler than a light saber?" he'll say wistfully, and it seems to make him so happy when his mom agrees that, yeah, when it comes to space-age swashbuckling, a light saber is pretty awesome, especially with that unmistakable electronic buzz. When one of those babies gets switched on, it's the sound of the good guys, and you know it's time to kick some evil Empire butt.

I think my son appreciates the stroke of good fortune that gave him a mom who understands his passion for this vast, imaginary world he can enter and explore at will. "Wow, Mom," he said the other day, "you're almost as big a *Star Wars* geek as I am," and I realized that, for him, this was a compliment of the highest order. After all, not everyone has a mom who can hold her own in a lengthy discussion about the merits of X-wing versus Y-wing spacecraft or the superior maneuverability of a tie-fighter. Or a mom who agrees wholeheartedly that "*I* am your father" is the greatest movie line—ever.

As for me, I just hope that when my son grows up and watches his old DVD's or pulls his Darth Vader mask out of a box in the attic, he'll smile and give me a call so we can laugh and reminisce about how much fun it was to love *Star Wars* together. Right now, though, the countdown to opening day has begun. When Anakin Skywalker succumbs to the Dark Side, my son and I will be there in the theater, wide-eyed with our popcorn. And as always, the *Force* will be with us.

TEENSPEAK

Consider, if you will, the following typical exchange between my teenage daughter and her best friend:

"Ohmygosh. Can you believe what that poser said in English today?!"
"I know. It was like, OUT OF CONTROL."
"Totally."
"Like, she *so* needs to get over herself."
"*Yeah*, she does."
"She's gotta know how lame she sounded."
"Or *not*."
"Well, anyway, it was seriously heinous."
"*Seriously*."

Now there was vital information shared here; I just don't know what it was. The fact is, however, that I'm not supposed to know. This is *their* language, a custom-made tool they have forged to help them build an identity apart from us. We did it, too. We all still do it, using language to create bridges, circles—sometimes walls.

When my daughter and her friends are talking, there's a rhythmic, almost percussive quality to their speech. It's all about nuance and tone and they play off of each other, creating their own brand of impromptu verbal jazz. In lighter moments, I find that I'm allowed to jam with them as long as I know my boundaries, as long as I know the music isn't mine.

Fortunately, there are a few words that are exempt from these lingual laws, words that are considered open season, even by sixteen-year-olds. *Cool* is one of them. The Clint Eastwood of with-it words, *cool* has been cool long enough to become a living legend. Consequently, if you're over forty, you can identify something as cool without fear of reprisals by someone under twenty. You *cannot*, however, say that something is *way cool*—unless of course you are kidding. There is a line we all must cross when it is no longer permissible to use a quantifier with *cool*, as in *way cool* or *majorly cool*. If you have to ask when this is, you have already crossed it.

Gross is another hall-of-famer and a personal favorite. I'm proud to say that *gross* came of age during my own teenage years and has yet to lose any of its original panache. In the early seventies, it was gross when we found my brother's pet hamster under a sofa cushion where it had taxidermied itself with the stuffing from a throw pillow. Thirty years later, that's as gross to my daughter and her ten-year-old brother as it was to me. Even the inflection remains the same. "Eww, gross!!" they wailed in unison upon hearing the tale. Eww, gross, indeed. That is staying power, the true hallmark of a classic.

So these days, as a captive audience in the kitchen or the carpool, I listen with fascination and a fair share of nostalgia to the unique patois of this current crop of teenagers. I listen for the birth of a new classic, something they can still own thirty years from now. But mostly, I listen to what they're *really* saying, knowing they'll never say it quite like this again.

WALTZING WITH RHETT

In retrospect, I can see that my senior prom was doomed from the start. Utterly besotted by *Gone with the Wind* since first seeing a re-release in the theater at the age of fourteen, I wanted nothing less for my high school swan song than the barbecue at *Twelve Oaks*. Most teenage girls obsess about something, but to this day, I am confounded by the length and breadth of my affliction, one that could not be assuaged by anything in *Tiger Beat* or *Seventeen* magazine, one not shared or even understood by any of my contemporaries.

While most of my classmates spent the weeks before the prom tanning with baby oil and aluminum reflectors and scoping the mall for the latest in sequins and spaghetti straps, I longed for a hoop skirt covered with yards of greensprigged white organdy, an emerald green ribbon cinched around my tiny corseted waist, and a floppy straw sun bonnet to shield my fair complexion and frame my flirtatious glances. And while the other girls mooned over Bobby Sherman, David Cassidy, and other wimpy boymen of a similar ilk, my hormones had cut their teeth on Clark Gable as Rhett Butler. Indeed, when I first saw the scene where he stands at the bottom of that winding staircase and watches Scarlett with that delicious, predatory grin, I experienced a pituitary surge that was probably akin to a drug overdose.

Never mind that the movie was already well over thirty years old by the time I saw it or that Clark Gable was born the same year as my grandfather and had died when I was three. To my incurably romantic imagination, Clark Gable's Rhett Butler was the ultimate in magnificent cads—sexy and dangerous, yet vulnerable and redeemable, too—and from the time I first laid eyes on him, I was suffused with a pure and terrible longing that would not be denied. It didn't even matter that by seventeen, I had read enough about Clark Gable to know that he had been an unrepentant womanizer with ill-fitting dentures and a weakness for raw onion sandwiches. In my world, he had perfect teeth; he smelled of leather, hand milled soap, and the outdoors, and no other woman existed for him but me. And how I longed for this paragon to appear at the bottom of the staircase of my teenage suburban life, resplendent in his snowy white cravat and billowing black evening cloak, ready to sweep me onto an antebellum dance floor in a sensory overload of candlelight, waltz music, and luxury fabrics.

But alas, this was 1975, the dawn of the disco years and the apex of the tackiest era in fashion history. It was a time of glistening flammable polyester, of stick-straight hair parted down the middle and accompanied by sullen expressions, of platform shoes and ruffly-shirted tuxedos the colors of sidewalk chalk. Even someone as possessed of a rich, anachronistic fantasy life as I was could do little in the face of such harsh reality as this.

Still, I tried. I found a pretty tiered dress of white dotted swiss and my mother fashioned a length of wide green velvet ribbon to tie around by decidedly uncorseted waist. My good-natured high school sweetheart did his best, showing up at my door in a powder blue tux and black vinyl slip-ons, a wilted corsage in hand. His hair was still damp from the shower, his cowlicks inexpertly tamped down.

We arrived at the ballroom of a mid-priced hotel in downtown Atlanta, ballroom being a euphemism, actually, for a cavernous space with gray institutional carpeting and movable room partitions folded accordion-style against the wall. This ambiance was tempered somewhat by a smattering of streamers and balloons, and by darkness and the obligatory revolving disco ball once the music started. We then spent the next several hours growing ever more sweaty and disheveled as we gyrated to the questionable rhythms of a less-than-stellar band. This was followed by a "midnight breakfast" consisting of rubbery scrambled eggs, greasy sausage, and crunchy biscuits served on Formica-topped tables under operating room-level fluorescent lighting. Shortly thereafter, my boyfriend took me home where we made out for a while in my driveway before I went inside to take a shower and go to bed. It was years before I could view this evening with any sense of equanimity as a valuable life lesson.

I have a seventeen-year-old daughter of my own now, a passionate, romantic young woman who is also adept at creating an elaborate virtual life for those times when reality does not suffice. That is lamentably often, it seems, and I feel her pain. She has an obsession of her own, of course. It is Clay Aiken and she is convinced that all she has to do is meet him and their mutual destiny will be sealed. And who am I to discourage her? From my perspective, marrying Clay seems perfectly do-able. At least he's still alive.

LAST BABY TOOTH

Why was that baby tooth so hard to pull last night? I didn't think it was quite ready, but you insisted. "Mom," you said—it was the day after you turned eleven—"it's really bugging me. Can't you just rip it out of there?"

"I don't want to hurt you," I said, wincing at the thought of the tugging. And the blood.

"I don't care if it hurts. It'll be worth it," you said, so I washed my hands and got a piece of paper towel for traction.

It really wasn't ready. I've always found it's best if one side has detached, providing some leverage. This one was still hanging on tight.

"Don't be afraid, Mom; just yank it. It's driving me crazy."

"Are you sure? I asked. "There's going to be a lot of blood."

"Yeah, Mom, I'm really, really a hundred percent sure."

"O.K., if you're sure. I mean, it's loose, but it's not *that* loose."

"C'mon, Mom; it's loose enough. And besides," you said, trying to talk around my fingers in your mouth, "it's the last one, and I just want to get it over with."

The last one. Even as I tugged, rocked it back and forth—felt it give way—I wanted to stop, wanted to shove it back in the socket and glue it in place. The last one. But it was too late. There it was, the last bit of your babyhood, held between my thumb and forefinger.

"Cool, Mom—you did it!" you said in triumph as I jammed the paper towel against your gum to stop all the blood I had predicted. "Let me see!"

Briefly, I curled my fingers over the tooth in my palm, clenched it in my fist, before letting it drop into your outstretched hand.

"Wow, the last one," you said, mumbling around the bloody paper towel. "Thanks, Mom; you tried really hard. I should get the big bucks for this one, shouldn't I? I didn't think it would ever let go."

THE ULTIMATE ROAD TRIP

Until recently, being young was all I had ever known. It was my familiar stomping grounds, no map required. Aging was a foreign country, one I had made no plans to visit, inhabited by people I could not relate to and had no real wish to know.

But I turned forty, then forty-two and forty-five, and gradually, I began to realize that I had somehow driven out of the old neighborhood and onto the entrance ramp of a busy interstate, one with heavy, fast-flowing traffic and no U-turns allowed. Given no choice but to merge and accelerate, I now find myself rushing along much faster than I'd like, the well-known scenery of my youth falling away behind me in the rear-view mirror, with nothing but uncharted territory ahead. And barreling along, the reality finally hits me, like a sudden cloudburst pelting the windshield. The end of the road lies somewhere out there and I am on my way to it.

As I set out on this rather unsettling journey into midlife and beyond, I can't help but remember when I was nine and my parents, who were medical professors at the University of North Carolina, decided it would be a great adventure to accept faculty positions at the University of New Mexico in Albuquerque, eighteen hundred miles away from everything I had ever known. Leaving behind a rambling white colonial and the leafy green idyll that was Chapel Hill in the sixties, my parents and their four children, all of us under the age of ten, piled into a 1965 Olds Cutlass and ventured westward to a land of flat-roofed adobes, barren mesas, and more open sky than I had ever dreamed of. Then, as now, I watched in some alarm as, over the course of our journey, a well-loved landscape gradually disappeared from view. The trip took three days and I recall how the trees seemed to retreat with every passing mile until we reached the Texas Panhandle and they were gone altogether, leaving me with a palpable sense of loss. My baby brother was a year old at the time and had just started walking the day the movers were emptying the house. Desperately unhappy at being confined to a car seat for nine hours at a stretch and unable to exercise his newfound skill, he kicked and screamed the whole way. I envied him his freedom of expression.

Of course, it turned out all right in the end. During the seven years that we lived in Albuquerque, I grew to love New Mexico and the Southwest, as so many people do, with a passion that has lasted to this day. Yes, I missed the trees of my southern childhood, but I soon discovered the cottonwood groves on the banks of the Rio Grande and the cool evergreen forests high in the Sangre de Cristo Mountains outside of Santa Fe.

I fell in love with the smell of piñon fires, the zest of green chiles, the clear, high desert nights lit by a star-filled sky. If we had not struck out for a new life in New Mexico, despite the fact that it was different and strange and scary, I might never have been awed by the sight of prehistoric cliff dwellings, their ancient walls warmed by a golden October morning. My life might never have been enriched by the wisdom and the art of the Hopi, the Zuni, or the Navajo people. I would not have the memory of dozens of hot air balloons rising from the desert into a cloudless turquoise sky. I would not associate Christmas Eve with the soft glow of thousands of handmade luminarias outlining every neighborhood street and adobe rooftop, creating magic. If it weren't for New Mexico, I would not be who I am today.

We moved back East when I was sixteen, but much of the *Land of Enchantment* resides within me still, as does that wary nine-year-old girl who left the familiar haven of a southern college town, so afraid that nothing would ever be the same. It wasn't, but it was good nonetheless.

That young girl travels with me now as we navigate this one-way road together. "Are we there yet?" she may ask, just as my siblings and I did so often on that long-ago trek.

No, thank goodness, we're not there yet, and I'll tell her to be patient because I plan to stop at as many scenic overlooks and explore as many hidden back roads as I can along the way, knowing full well that eventually, they will all lead me to the same destination.

Already the headlights have grown a bit dimmer, the alignment is a little out-of-whack and there's an ever-increasing amount of baggage in the trunk, but as long as the open road still beckons, something tells me that the best part of the journey lies ahead.

THE WAY THE LIGHT
SHINES THROUGH

CALL IT LIKE IT IS

For years, I've had a love-hate relationship with cell phones. I'm glad I've got one in my purse in case my car breaks down or my children need me. And it's nice to know that I don't have to touch those grungy pay phones anymore, the ones that always smell funny and are grimy with substances of unknown origin. Besides, you can hardly find a working pay phone anymore, even if you wanted one.

But as much as I rely on my cell phone and wonder how I ever got along without it, I have to marvel at our rapid and somewhat bizarre evolution into a nation of cell phone dependents. It is no longer unusual to hear women chatting away in public restroom stalls or to see men switching their phones from ear to ear while sitting in the barber chair. And my friends and I trade stories about how often we are entertained by half-conversations of a most intimate and revelatory nature while waiting in line at the post office, the bank, or Burger King. It's almost as if people believe that their cell phones come with a built-in soundproof bubble, a sort of invisible phone booth enabling them to speak without being heard by anyone nearby.

Quite frequently, I've found myself becoming a bit surly and judgmental when it comes to poor cell phone behavior because it's really nothing more than plain old bad manners. But although I'll always be annoyed whenever I see people in restaurants carrying on animated phone conversations while their lunch partners fiddle with the salad fork, I have to say that after September 11, my attitude, like so much else in our lives, changed for good.

How could we have foreseen that this palm-sized status symbol that we clip to our belts and decorate with silly neon and cow print covers would, after that horrible Tuesday, find itself draped in a mantle of bravery and valor? Yet over and over again in the aftermath of that tragedy, we heard about the role cell phones played in allowing loved ones to make a final, desperate connection. Many of us have voice-activated phones now. How many people, faced with terror we cannot begin to imagine, their fingers trembling too hard to press the buttons, simply held the phone to their mouths and whispered, "Home"?

I am still haunted by the story of the husband who called from one of the hijacked planes to tell his wife to have a good life and to take care of their baby girl. His phone allowed them both this heartrending, yet priceless benediction to their life together. Without cell phones, we might never have known about the passengers on the Pittsburgh flight who, in the face of certain death, said, "We are going to do something about this." That plane didn't hit its intended target. Because of cell phones, we're pretty sure we know why.

We do use our cell phones too much, for too many trivial things. I still don't think we should talk and drive at the same time or take calls in church or at the movies. But in general, it's going to be hard to muster as much outrage as I used to, because after that Tuesday, I will never again look at my cell phone in quite the same way.

I pray to God I'll never have to use my phone like so many did on that unthinkable day, to say, "I love you" and "goodbye" for the very last time. But from now on, every time I call my husband somewhere on a business trip or text my kids to let them know I'm running late, I will no longer take for granted the true power of this little machine in my hand.

I will not overlook the wonder of how, across the physical mysteries of time and space, radio waves travel from one tiny point to another. Like fireflies signaling each other in the summer twilight, or a whale sending its song across a fathomless expanse of ocean, we send out signals of our own. Most of them are drowned out and forgotten in the everyday noise of life. But some of them make all the difference.

MY BROTHER'S GIFT

As children, my brother Rob and I were never close. We didn't fight; we just ignored each other. I was the bookish dreamer, never so happy as when I was holed up in some corner with my latest prize from the library. My dyslexic brother, on the other hand, considered the written word his enemy. Early on, he gave up trying to put words together with his eyes and turned instead to putting things together with his hands. To this day, he would rather not follow an instruction manual. Yet he can take a burnt-out toaster or a junkyard heap and, as if by instinct, bring it back to life.

Our one shared passion through the years has been our love of old things, especially those that tie us to our family history, and to our paternal grandmother in particular. Grandma was a sweet, eccentric soul of pure English descent who made the best tea I've ever tasted and who never seemed quite comfortable with life in the twentieth century. She and Grandpa lived far away in Ohio, but she was a dedicated correspondent, writing us wonderful, copious letters, always typed, in her unique stream-of-consciousness style. The lines often went uphill and downhill on the same page and would sometimes even overlap each other. She loved birds and would write to us about the "morning doves" in her backyard, always spelling them without the "u" in "mourning." She once wrote that she wondered why they were called that since she saw them all day long.

My brother loved her fiercely and when she died suddenly at eighty-six, in the same house she had come to as a bride, my sister-in-law told me that this man who never cries locked himself in their bedroom and sobbed for hours.

It was my brother who later took time off from work and drove to Ohio to sift through all that our grandmother had hoarded during her more than sixty years in that house. She had lived alone for a decade after Grandpa died, and much of what my brother had hoped to rescue before the estate sale had already disappeared. Still, he came home with a truckload of boxes.

There was a large box for me under the tree that Christmas. I was surprised to see that it was not wrapped with my sister-in-law's department store precision, but rather in the half-dressed, off-kilter way of someone who has thrown on a bathrobe to answer the door. As I opened it, I could already smell the oldness of the thing inside—old metal, old rubber, old ink. It was Grandma's ancient manual typewriter; yet it looked as polished and ready-for-action as it must have when it was new. There was a piece of paper sticking out of the top with a message that read, "Merry Christmas from your brother." It was typed in red ink in a line going uphill.

DECIPHERING THE ZEROES

Written for the Turn of the Millennium

When I was growing up in Albuquerque in the late 1960s, summer vacation meant only one thing—road trips. My father, ordinarily an unassuming, bespectacled pediatrician and medical school professor, harbored a passion for the wide-open highways of the desert Southwest. At an early age, I realized that he was obsessed with covering every square inch of paved road from Carlsbad to Denver, from Phoenix to Tucumcari. And he was determined that his offspring would cover it with him.

Within days after school let out in June, he piled the four of us—my two brothers, my sister and me, the oldest—into his mammoth two-door Olds 98 and we took off on the first of several week-long summer adventures. Our mother, also a busy pediatrician and faculty member, invariably found some compelling reason to stay behind. Usually, it was a quiet house and a stack of good books. Truth be told, her reluctance to join us was also the sign of a deeply troubled marriage, but as a kid, I was still trying hard to be oblivious to such implications.

Perhaps due to his line of work, my father seemed undaunted by the prospect of spending a week at a time traveling the Southwest with four children under the age of twelve. The youngest, my baby brother Fred, was still in a car seat when he began to come along. The seat in question, however, was not one of those federally-approved child restraint systems. On the contrary, it was little more than a booster chair with armrests and aluminum brackets that hooked over the middle of the front seat. The belt, a thin plastic strap, was similar to the kind found on grocery store shopping carts. It is a testament to guardian angels and to my father's driving skills that little Fred survived into adulthood considering his potential for becoming a human projectile.

Every year, it was obvious that Dad could hardly wait to hit the road. The first warm spring evenings found him out on the screened porch in his plaid shorts, a crisp new Rand McNally road atlas spread out on the wrought iron picnic table. By the beginning of May, he had every trip planned out to the minutest detail and somehow we knew that any input regarding possible destinations or points of interest was neither expected nor welcome. All we had to do was take our Dramamine, hop in the car, and go.

To my father's credit, we covered a lot of ground during those long-ago summers, gaining a tremendous education in the process. Whether it was Carlsbad Caverns, White Sands, Mesa Verde, or Pike's Peak, Dad made sure we understood exactly where we were and what we were experiencing. Ironically, despite his own insatiable wanderlust, he instilled in us a strong sense of place, and for that I will always be grateful.

When I look back on those trips now, though, I remember not so much the destinations as the journeys themselves, that Charles Kuralt feeling of being "on the road." In those days, there were no speed limits on the open mesas of New

Mexico or Colorado. The goal was simply to put miles behind you as quickly as possible. And why not, since it was not uncommon to be able to see fifty miles in a straight line both coming and going. Picking up on our dad's love of speed, we urged him on, yelling, "Faster, faster!" as he gunned his big old tank across some empty stretch of highway, the Rockies almost always towering somewhere in the distance like a huge benevolent compass point. We could easily hit ninety-five before the V-8 even started vibrating.

Dad had a thing about the odometer, too. He loved to see the zeroes come up every thousand miles. Ten thousand miles and it was a major event. There would be twenty miles to go and he'd already be preparing us. But then, at ninety miles per hour, it was only a fifteen-minute wait.

"Get ready," he'd say and we'd all lean forward, crowding over his shoulder to watch the nines start inching upwards. "Here we go; here we go," he'd continue somewhat breathlessly, and we never stopped to think that it might be better if he were watching the road instead of the dashboard. He was like a kid about the whole thing, but since the four of us were the genuine article, we had no trouble buying into his enthusiasm.

Ultimately, whether we were watching the numbers or not, we always knew when the climactic moment had arrived because Dad would begin to slow down. "Don't miss it!" he'd shout, "Here come all the zeroes!" Of course, no sooner did he say this than his perfect line of ciphers was already being marred by the rapidly advancing tenths, their advancement being made only slightly less rapid by his deceleration from ninety to sixty-five. "There they go," he would sigh with either contentment or resignation, then step on the gas again as we settled back into our seats. I still remember feeling strangely invigorated by these experiences because, instinctively, I understood something about my father even then. His zeroed-out odometer was a clean slate, a chance, however brief, to start over, even in the middle of nowhere.

I've thought about my dad and his odometer a lot lately as I've tried to make sense of the hype surrounding the end of this year. The purists who insist that the millennium doesn't really start until January 1, 2001, are missing the point. They'll never get people to wait until then for the mother of all celebrations. We need the big round number, the line of nines marching into oblivion, the band of circles rolling cleanly into view. 2001? Forget it; there aren't enough zeroes.

Yet friends are already asking me, "What are you doing for New Year's Eve?" They sound somewhat at a loss, as if desperate for a suggestion on how to do it justice, to make it BIG enough. I don't know what to tell them. How do you celebrate the rounding off of two thousand years? Right now, I'd be happy just to know that I'll have running water and electricity on New Year's Day.

In the end, I guess it doesn't matter where I am or what I'm doing as midnight approaches this December 31st. All I really want is to feel the same way I felt as a kid when my dad opened it up on some lonely New Mexico straightaway, the engine roaring in our ears, the high desert falling away behind us. I want to feel the same way he felt when he came up on all those zeroes and slowed down, just long enough to make them mean something.

IRONING IT OUT

Mattie was usually ironing when I got home from school. In the winter, especially, she liked to save that chore until the end of the day, so she could set up my mother's ironing board in front of the sliding glass door in the breakfast room and stand in the warmth of the afternoon sun. Mattie once told me that she liked to iron and now, years later, as a busy mother of two, I wonder if my bounding through the back door at four o'clock put a boisterous end to an all-too-rare period of sanctuary in her day. If it did, she never let on, always welcoming me, my two younger brothers, and my little sister as if we were her own.

As a pediatrician with four kids and a demanding career, my mother needed help, and in the South of the sixties and seventies, that help still came in the form of legions of black women who rode buses away from their own homes five days a week to work for affluent white families in the suburbs. From the time my siblings and I were born, our lives were greatly influenced by a series of Monday-through-Friday surrogate mothers who helped our mother raise us. These strong, nurturing women cleaned our house, washed our clothes, bandaged our knees, taught us manners, and loved us—just as we loved them. As children, we accepted this arrangement without question. It was simply the way things were. It was not until I was older that I began to understand how my mother had wrestled with the whole scenario from the very beginning.

A woman who had dreamed of becoming a doctor since childhood, my mother had learned a thing or two about discrimination and "knowing her place." During the process of applying to medical school, she was interviewed by a dean who told her to give up her "girlish whim" and marry a doctor instead. Of course, spitfire that she was, this only fanned the flames of her ambition. Her aversion to inequality or subservience of any sort became a double-edged sword, however, when she became a mother and found it difficult to reconcile her desire for a professional career with the very real need for household help. Only by creating a firm set of guidelines for the situation was she able to soothe her conscience enough to make it palatable.

The word *maid* was not permitted in our house. *Nanny* and *housekeeper* were allowed, but only because they had a slightly less offensive connotation in my mother's mind. She absolutely cringed at being called "ma'am" and I recall her repeated attempts to stamp out that word in her hearing as if it were some pesky, crackling brushfire. If she had found a way to do it, I'm sure she would have created some sort of utopian communal arrangement, unsullied by the whole employer/employee hierarchy.

Mattie was our last housekeeper and by the time she came to work in our home, I was a teenager who had absorbed a great deal of my mother's idealistic zeal. Having been fully versed in the ongoing struggles of the Civil Rights Movement, I was filled to overflowing with a sixteen-year-old's self-righteous earnestness. The term "politically correct" had not been coined yet, but I'm sure that's what I was trying very hard to be.

When I got home from school, I would often ask Mattie, out of an ever-growing sense of guilt, if there was anything I could do for her while she ironed. Could I get her a glass of ice water? Would she like me to carry the folded laundry upstairs? Did she need a snack? She must have found all this amusing and maybe a little annoying, too, since one day, she finally said, "Honey, your mama hired me to do the housework, so that's what you got to let me do. If you want to do something, why don't you just sit here in the kitchen and keep me company. I'd like that."

And that's how my education started, sitting on the kitchen counter, long legs dangling, listening to Mattie's stories. Six feet tall and part Cherokee, Mattie was a compelling presence. She was also a born storyteller. It wasn't long before I was eagerly anticipating our "kitchen time" and the more we talked, the more I learned about what it was really like to live as a black woman in the mid-century South.

"You, know, child," she said to me one day, "we could wash your dishes; we could cook in your dishes, but there ain't no way we was gonna be eatin' or drinkin' out of 'em."

"That's just stupid," I remember saying with all the adolescent ardor I had in me, and from then on, I fixed her a glass of ice water every day whether she wanted it or not. It became a sort of sacred act between us and perhaps an act of penance for me.

I don't think Mattie had ever had an audience quite like me before and I'm not sure she knew what to make of it at first. "It ain't been all that long ago, we wouldn't a been havin' this conversation," she said once, shaking her head at the apparent novelty of it all. While I spent a lot of time getting riled up over many of the things Mattie told me, the truth of that statement just made me sad.

As time went on, I began to understand that Mattie had seen fit to entrust me not only with her stories, but with her secrets, and some of her deepest wounds. I can only hope that I was as humbled by this as I should have been. I do know that the more she told me, the more emboldened I became to know more. I was not prepared, however, for just how painful such knowledge could be.

One day, I asked her what she did for lunch in the days when she wasn't allowed to eat in the kitchens where she worked.

"Oh, you could *eat* in the kitchen," she said, "long as no one else was in there and long as you brought everything from home and ate it right out of the sack. I remember one time, though, when I forgot to bring something, and by two o'clock, I was so hungry, I couldn't hardly see straight."

"Couldn't you just explain that you forgot your lunch and ask for something to eat?"

"Well, honey, you know, that's just what I did. I asked the woman I worked for was there anything I could fix and just eat it off a napkin or something, and she says, 'Oh, don't worry about that; I'll fix you a bologna sandwich.'

"Well, I kept ironing and kept waiting for that sandwich 'til finally I figured she just done forgot about it."

"Did she?" I asked.

"No, sugar, she didn't forget." Mattie set the iron on its heel, causing a fresh burst of steam to hiss upwards towards the ceiling. "She come into the room a little while later and ask me, 'Don't you want that sandwich I fixed you?'

"I says to her, 'I'm sorry, ma'am, but I ain't seen no sandwich.' And she says, 'Well, I fixed it and set it outside for you.'"

Mattie leaned forward then, placing both palms on the ironing board, her hands dark against the white cotton of my father's dress shirt. "Do you know where that sandwich was, child?"

I shook my head, and I still remember the way my breath hitched in my chest because I knew the answer wasn't going to be good.

"I opened the back door thinkin' she had put it out there on the picnic table, but there wasn't nothin' on that picnic table, honey. That's when I looked down on the back stoop and seen it settin' there in the dog dish."

For a long, long moment, I looked at Mattie across the length of the kitchen, feeling as though a bridge had washed out, leaving us stranded on either side. Goosebumps covered every inch of my body and I had never been so aware of the color of my skin.

"Oh, Mattie," I whispered finally, dropping my gaze to my lap, "I am so sorry… I am just so, so sorry."

"Honey, you listen to me," she said in her strong storyteller voice. "It won't do you no good to feel guilty. What's past is past and you got to learn from what I been tellin' you. That's the only way things is gonna change."

I knew she was right, but it did little to loosen the knot of rage and shame that had lodged itself somewhere in my belly. "Please, Mattie," I said, "please tell me that you walked right out of that house and slammed the door."

She picked up the iron again, shaking her head. "Oh, baby, I can see you still got a lot to learn." Looking down at the ironing board, she began to press my father's shirt with long, firm strokes. "This was twenty years ago in Atlanta, Georgia, and I needed to get paid. You think some uppity colored woman was gonna get her pay handed to her while she went stompin' out the door in a hissy fit?"

"But you just couldn't have gone back to work for that horrible woman," I insisted, on the verge of a hissy fit of my own. "She shouldn't have gotten away with that."

"No, honey, she shouldn't, but folks has gotten away with a whole lot worse than that and you know it." Still looking down at her ironing,

Mattie smiled a little then, more to herself than me. "I didn't go back there, though, and sure enough, that ol' woman called me the next day, askin' me why didn't I show up for work. And you know what I told her? I said, 'Well, if you don't know, I sure ain't gonna tell you.'"

To this day, the clean, humid smell of steam, damp cotton, and spray starch never fails to remind me of an untouched sandwich in a dirty dog dish on a nameless back stoop in Georgia. But it also reminds me of the girl I was, sitting in a warm kitchen, legs swinging from the counter, as a proud woman and one of my best teachers pulled my father's rumpled shirts from the laundry basket and one by one, transformed them into something smooth and bright and unblemished.

STRANDS OF MEMORY

The hairbrush is probably thirty years old. It is not an heirloom by any means, just a drugstore variety plastic brush with nylon bristles, many of which have long since broken off, leaving uneven little tufts here and there, like the scalp of a man using Rogaine. I used this brush all through junior high, high school, and college when it lived at the bottom of various purses, along with pens, gum, lip gloss, and tampons, all those things considered basic equipment for adolescent girls.

I still keep this brush in my purse, and as long as it has a bristle in its gnarled plastic head, I always will. There has never been a hairbrush in my life before or since that has brushed my hair the way this one does, no brush that feels as good as I pull it through, or fluffs up my hair in as satisfying a way. It was and is my talisman against bad hair days.

This brush feels the same in my hand as it did when I was fourteen and thought I would die of love for Frank, the smart, handsome, tennis-playing boy in my journalism class. I would run to the girls' room on my way to fifth period every afternoon, brush my curly, waist-length hair over my head, then toss it back and check myself out in the old, wavy mirror with its rusted chrome frame and the dark splotches I had to look between. With this brush in my hand, I still see that primping girl with her fresh, hopeful face and all that soft, tumbling blond hair she took for granted.

I remember how that bathroom smelled, of borax and dusty radiators, of cheap, rough paper towels that reeked of wet cardboard. There was little to look at beyond the color gray—the stalls, hiding a row of black-seated toilets, the trash bins with their rusty, swinging lids, even the grout between the small square floor tiles, dirtied to the color of stone.

We were the color, the girls who poured in and out, laughing, gossiping, complaining—of teachers, of cramps, of our own images as we peered into those distorted old mirrors. We glossed; we powdered; but mostly we brushed, Samson-like in our belief in the power of our hair. I don't use this brush very often any more, mainly because I want it to last forever. I want to be able to use it when I'm an old woman. I hope I'll have good hair then, hair with some heft to it, hair I can still pull that brush through and feel some resistance, some spring.

Looking in the mirror, that brush in my hand, I will see that smiling, clear-eyed girl, tossing her mane back like a spirited colt, wondering for the first time if she really might be pretty, and wanting—wanting so much—for the world to notice her.

IT GOES RIGHT OVER OUR HEADS

Becoming an astronaut was not my destiny. I'm too claustrophobic, for starters, and advanced math was never my thing. But that didn't stop me from developing a lifelong fascination with all things space-related. I'm one of those people who keeps track of the phases of the moon, the seasonal positions of Mars and Venus, and the likelihood of a meteor shower. It sounds paradoxical, I know, but for me, there's something comforting about the unfathomability of it all.

Naturally, it makes my day whenever the local paper announces that the International Space Station will be passing through our celestial neighborhood. By now, my husband and kids are used to seeing a sticky note appear on the kitchen cabinet every few weeks reminding me of the exact time and coordinates of the next fly-over. Shaking their heads, they smile indulgently as I bundle up before dawn or leave dinner on the stove in order to keep my regular five-minute rendezvous at the end of our driveway. Sometimes, if it's not too early or too cold—or if the TV isn't too mesmerizing—they join me, and I keep hoping my cosmic cheerleading will rub off on them.

We tend to get ourselves so revved up over the stuff that's shoved in our faces every day— the latest sports statistics, the latest *American Idol* auditions, the latest antics of Brad and Angelina. For me, those few moments spent in the dark, waiting for a fast-moving pinpoint of light to climb out of the horizon, provide a wake-up call, a welcome reminder of what's *really* amazing.

Every once in a while, it just feels good to marvel, to stand in awe, not only of the universe, but of the collective earthly intelligence that vaulted a house-sized metal contraption into orbit and enables human beings to live and work on it for six months at a time. There are *people* up there, I think every time I see it, and I get goosebumps still. What do they see, I wonder, as they streak across the night sky, sometimes threading right through the notches in Orion's belt. The whole east coast of North America, at least, its cities mapped out in lights, and all of it bumped up against the vast darkness of the Atlantic.

A Saudi Arabian astronaut on the space shuttle once said that "on the first day, we all pointed to our countries. The third or fourth day, we were pointing to our continents. By the fifth day, we were aware of only one Earth." The rest of us will never have that stunning perspective of our planet, but I think it would do us all a lot of good to step outside in the deepening twilight every now and then and watch for the ones who do. After all, watching them watching us can't help but make our own world view a little bigger.

STUFFED

There was an article in the local newspaper recently about a highly successful guy in Charlotte who makes his living by hauling people's junk away. He says the average fee for his service runs about three hundred bucks a pop and with the way things are going, he expects to have a multimillion-dollar business within the next year or so. It's hard, sweaty work, of course, but he and his crew sounded pretty chipper about it. Seems the sky's the limit when it comes to people who will pay to have their old stuff taken off their hands.

I'm happy for the guy. I really am. But I can't help feeling it's a shame that, as a society, we've become *stuffed* to the gills. All over town, I see an endless proliferation of guarded, climate-controlled storage facilities. Space we're willing to rent to hold the stuff we can't part with, but don't have room for at home. And for the stuff that does live with us, there are places like Target and Walmart that devote entire departments to plastic boxes, rolling drawers, stackable bins, baskets, trunks—even sheds. Because naturally, we need loads of stuff to put our stuff in.

When you think about it, isn't it our stuff that keeps us so busy? Don't most of our errands revolve around it? Running hither and yon, we're either fixing it, cleaning it, moving it, or buying more of it. And back at home, our lives become an endless loop of sorting, sifting, organizing, rearranging, and culling. Honestly, don't the most heinous chores on those Saturday to-do lists usually have something to do with closets, basements, or garages? Think of the attention we lavish on our stuff that we could devote to other things. Like people, for instance.

We drag stuff with us on vacation, too, despite our professed desire to get away from it all. But could it be that, deep down, we love going to the beach because when we're standing on an empty stretch of sand at sunset, staring at the ocean, there's an absence of stuff as far as the eye can see? Same thing with the mountains.

High on the Blue Ridge Parkway, gazing down on those sunny green valleys, we see only good stuff—like grass and trees and maybe a lone hawk soaring. Of course, a lot of our stuff is precious. Old photos, your great-grandparents' mahogany headboard, that lock of curls from your baby's first haircut. And when I think of natural disasters like Hurricane Katrina and the countless people who lost everything, I have to be honest. I still want to be in control of my stuff despite its frequent stranglehold on me. But I also can't help wondering about that old expression, "less is more." No, really, I want to say; that's OK. Less doesn't have to be more. Wouldn't we all be a lot happier if less could just be less?

THE POWER OF PIE

One summer, while vacationing in the northern Rockies, my family and I stopped for lunch at a ramshackle cottage just outside the entrance to Glacier National Park. According to our guidebook, people had been flocking there for over twenty years—mainly for the pie. The restaurant even had its own T-shirts for sale, emblazoned with a giant wedge of berry pie and accompanied by the inspiring slogan, "Pie for Strength." Naturally, I bought one, not only because it made a nifty souvenir, but because I had finally found the perfect family motto.

I descend from a long line of illustrious pie makers. My mother's pie, like her mother's and grandmother's before her, can bring a grown man to his knees. Upon sampling the first bite of, say, her lemon meringue or pecan, the blessed individual will invariably be compelled to set his fork down and groan in culinary ecstasy. He will know he has reached pie Nirvana and it is good.

Indeed, as an heir to this legacy, I couldn't feel that I had earned the family pie plate of approval until some unwitting guest partook of one of my creations and was moved to say, "You made this?!" "From scratch?!" Only then could I smile that secret—yes, even smug—little smile, knowing that the pie genes had been conferred upon the next generation.

We are admitted pie snobs, my mother, my sister, and I. No frozen or refrigerated crusts for us, no plastic-wrapped disks from the dairy case to be unfolded, slapped into a pie plate, and filled with some unmentionable goo from a can. That is pseudo-pie, unworthy of the name. Like tomatoes in January or Chopin on a synthesizer.

I've never understood the expression "as easy as pie." Real pie isn't all that easy. It's a skill well worth mastering, however, if only to free you from the helpless feeling of pie envy. Nevertheless, I have encountered any number of people who, despite an unholy craving for a slab of strawberry-rhubarb, are actually afraid of pie-making, as if it is some elusive skill beyond the reach of mortals. I must admit that I am OK with this. There's no denying the seductive thrill of having the topic of pie come up and hearing people murmur with drool and longing, "But have you tasted *her* pie? It's an out-of-body experience."

Over the years, I've encouraged my two children to sample pies of every ilk, from the sacred to the profane, in an effort to fine-tune their palates and prepare them for the mantle that will be handed down. Aware of this awesome responsibility, they've become adept at discerning a leaden crust or a canned filling on sight. Someday soon, they will be ready to weave a lattice top of their own.

Oh, and the blackberry pie at that little café in Montana? It was quite good, we all agreed, but not as good as mine.

THE BEAUTY IN THE BEAST

The appraiser at my grandmother's estate sale said I couldn't get three hundred dollars for it. "It'll cost you more to move it than it's worth," he said, incredulous at my plan to ship the old piano from Grandma's house in Cleveland, Ohio, to my home in Milwaukee, Wisconsin.

I could see his point. A truly hideous upright, it was caked with layers of black paint and hopelessly out of tune, a great hulking thing with chipped ivory keys resembling the yellowed, broken teeth of an aging draft horse. But the Beast, as I had by then dubbed it, once belonged to my great grandfather, my paternal grandmother's beloved "Papa" who had died decades before. By all accounts a kind and exceedingly loving man, he was also an

Episcopalian priest and a gifted musician who had used this piano to compose hymns and musical morality plays for his congregation during the early part of the twentieth century. My grandmother, a rather wistful and melancholy woman, inherited none of her father's musical talent, but lit up whenever she spoke of his. Her childhood in the manse where she lived with her parents and four siblings was filled with music and laughter. She made it sound like an idyllic time, probably the best time of her eighty-six years.

Even though the piano sat unplayed in her cramped dining room for half a century, I knew that it served as a comforting, if silent, reminder of her Papa and his music. I think I knew, too, why she wanted me to have it. I'd been a bit more generously blessed with musical genes than either she or my father had, and after the obligatory childhood lessons, had learned to play the piano passably well. More than that, though, it was likely Grandma's first impression of me that had stayed with her for thirty years. "Look at those long fingers," she said to my parents just after I was born. "They were made for piano playing—just like Papa's." So in the end, though

I might regret caring for the Beast for the rest of my life, there was no way I could let it leave the family, no way it was going to languish in some damp church basement, its history unknown.

Several weeks later, a moving van deposited the sorry creature at my address, and after watching four strapping men wrestle all twelve hundred pounds of it up the front steps and through the door, I couldn't help but ask myself what I had done. If anything, it looked worse in my bright, airy living room than it had in Grandma's dreary sixty-year-old house. By then, however, I had a new baby and a husband who was pondering a cross-country job transfer, so I had no choice but to leave the Beast in its forlorn and neglected state until I could find the time and energy to deal with it.

My husband accepted the new position a few months later and, along with all our other worldly goods, the Beast made yet another road trip to our new home in Raleigh, North Carolina. This time, I took one look at that dark monstrosity settled against one of the pristine white walls in my newly constructed colonial and promptly called one of the two piano refurbishers listed in the yellow pages. A raspy, no-nonsense voice answered the phone and although the man sounded dubious when I described the challenge at hand, he agreed to come by and take a look. A few days later, I came to the door to find a tall, spindly-looking fellow stomping out a cigarette butt on my front porch. "Bad habit," he said, looking up. "So— let's see what you've got."

Feeling somewhat wary, I led him to the obvious eyesore. He studied it for a moment, then hunkered down, pulling out a pocketknife. I watched as he began scraping at the paint on the back of one leg. "Hmmm," he said, suddenly interested. "Do you know what you have here?" To be honest, I felt intimidated by this man's gruff intensity, not to mention his choking aura of tobacco, and since it was obvious I didn't know what I had, I just looked at him and shook my head.

"This is tiger oak," he said, his eyes now alight with a kind of artistic fire. "You never see this wood grain anymore." He continued to scrape large flakes of black paint onto my cream-colored carpet, shaking his head in wonder, like an archeologist uncovering a dinosaur bone. After a time, he seemed to will himself to stop scraping and stood up. "I'll be honest with you," he said, putting the knife back in his pocket and fishing for a cigarette. "This is going to cost you some money. I'll have to gut this thing, strip it bare, and rebuild it from the inside out, but I do good work—you can ask anybody—and I guarantee you'll have a prize when I'm done."

Maybe it was his honest confidence, or maybe it was the longing in his eyes as he gazed at the patch of beautiful wood he had just revealed, but something told me I could trust him. I decided then and there to use most of the lump sum of cash my grandmother had left me and give him the job. It would be, after all, like giving the money back to her.

He arranged to have the Beast carted off to his workshop and over the next three months, he called every once in a while with rather vague progress reports. "She's coming along," he'd say, or "She's looking good; shouldn't be much longer." I might have grown concerned if it weren't for the unmistakable note of excitement in his smoky voice, as if he were kindling a wonderful secret.

When the day finally came for the piano to be delivered, I was like a child at Christmas, barely able to contain my own anticipation. It was a little before noon when he pulled into the driveway in a rented truck with the three men he had hired to help him. I stood on the lawn, transfixed, as they opened the rear doors, set up the ramp, and slowly rolled the piano out of the shadows and into the sunlight. At first glance, I thought there had to be some mistake. This could not possibly be the same piano that had left my house just a few months before.

In its place was a vision of honey-gold wood, the subtle tiger-stripe grain he had referred to now burnished and gleaming in the late morning light. The intricate scrollwork on the front panel that had been buried under layers of paint now stood out in bold relief above a sparkling new keyboard. After a few stunned moments, I realized that the man responsible for this miracle was watching my reaction and as I met his gaze, the tears I had tried to hold back began in earnest. Since I was speechless, it was the most eloquent response I could offer.

When the piano was once again settled against my living room wall (now looking as though it belonged there), the other men went outside to wait, but he stepped back, motioning for me to play something. Slightly embarrassed, but unable to refuse him, I began to play the old piano student standby, Beethoven's "Für Elise." After so many years without a piano, it was the only piece I still knew by heart. The sound was sweet, warm, and full, the keys strong and solid beneath my fingers. He had warned me it would never be a Steinway, but then, it didn't need to be. This was already beyond anything I could have hoped for, and I vowed I would learn to play again, if only to do it justice.

"Do you think you might be able to finish a bench to match?" I asked as I handed him his hefty, but well-deserved check. Belatedly, I realized that the rickety stool that had come with the piano could no longer remain alongside this magnificent instrument.

"Don't think I'll have time for that," he said, fumbling in his shirt pocket for his next smoke.

"Oh," I said, disappointed. I couldn't see anyone else taking over now. "I can understand why you'd have more business than you can handle."

He looked at me, a bit taken aback. "Oh, no; it's not that," he said. "The cancer's come back." He paused, rolling the unlit cigarette between his stained fingers. "Don't ever smoke," he said, without a trace of self-pity.

I never saw him again, but I imagine that mine was the last piano he brought back to life. I imagine, too, that he left a part of his soul in it.

Just as my grandmother did.

Just as her Papa did.

Just as I will.

DON'T SAY

Don't say it's a shame that the last family
picture with my grandmother is the one where
someone's eyes are closed. Or complain about
the squeaky stairs. Why would I fix them when
they tell me you've come home? Let's talk
instead about the dog and the pointed ear that
falls over one eye like tired origami, the click of
her nails across the wooden floor, and the nudge
of her unpedigreed nose when you sit with your
head in your hands. Let's take mugs of good
coffee up to the dusty attic with its crumbling old
dirt dauber nest under the eaves. We'll sit on the
frayed German quilt that survived an Atlantic
crossing in steerage and sift through the box of
yellowed love letters your parents exchanged. At
lunch, we'll laugh at the brazen squirrel who
waits by the back door for stale bread, the one

we know by his bent tail and the bald patch on his belly. When the kids get home from school, we can go for a drive beneath the leaden sky, past the old barn in the stubbled field, the rolls of hay rimmed in frost. We'll sing with the radio, and despite the grayness, something will remind me of Mother's Day dandelions, of paint-dribbled handprints, of misspelled words, and backward S's. Never mind the brewing storm. Just think of the warm kitchen when we all dash in laughing with dripping umbrellas and muddy shoes. Right now, I don't need to know what it takes to be a saint. Let me wonder about the wedding glass crushed underfoot, the dove returning with an olive branch, *my body broken for you*. When heaven comes, I'll be glad for an end to suffering, loss, and grief. But tell me there will still be low-slung clouds and beaches strewn with driftwood come to rest. Or worn stone benches tucked along a narrow wooded path. Won't I need a place of dappled shadow where I can sit and remember how the light shone through?

MAKE A JOYFUL NOISE

Though I've always loved to sing, I knew early on that divahood was not for me. A shy child, I could not imagine singing by myself in front of people. Instead, I sang in my room or alone as I walked home from school. Only my mother, a singer too, knew of my secret passion and put me in the children's choir at church where, looking cherubic, we produced an enthusiastic cacophony of voices in varying degrees of pitch. But it was not until seventh grade, when I took a junior high chorus elective with an extraordinary music teacher, that I realized that children singing together could actually sound good, could create, in fact, something akin to magic. From that point on, my choral destiny was sealed and aside from a few brief and dismal interludes, I have been in a choir ever since.

There is a feeling of safety in singing with other people. There is also strength and an inexplicable power. I often contemplate the profound spiritual impact that choral singing has had upon my life, how it adds immeasurably to times of joy, how it buoys me up in times of pain.

Over the years, I have kept singing, through the struggles of adolescence and the heady years of college when fellow singers became lifelong friends. I have sung through courtship and marriage, having fallen in love with a tenor in my church choir. I have sung through the heartache of my parents' divorce and my father's disappearance from my life. I have sung through a miscarriage and two healthy pregnancies, returning to rehearsal a week after my babies were born because I couldn't stay away. And I sang through my sister's cancer and recovery— and later my own—when singing was one of the few things that kept me sane.

I sing now, as I always have, for peace, for comfort, and as an expression of my faith, but also for those incomparable moments of unity with other human beings, for the pure, unfettered joy that comes when somehow, the sound we are creating becomes greater than the sum of its parts. Those moments are what we singers live for. It doesn't matter if it's the clean, precise finish of a Bach motet, the sonorous minor chords of a Russian Orthodox hymn, or the soaring finale of a gospel Mass. Like a school of silver minnows that shifts and shimmers in unison against an invisible current, or a flock of geese that descends in perfect V-formation upon the still waters of a pond, we strive toward a oneness, a point where we are utterly attuned to each other. Such moments are rare, but they come, often when we least expect them. As if following an unseen lead, we arrive at a chord that is so rich and so true, we feel it resonate all the way down to our toes. No longer merely making music, we have *become* it. And it is then that we know, beyond a doubt, that God is real, that life is sweet, that we are not alone.

STAYING AFLOAT

For beachcombers along the northwest Pacific coast, there is no find more precious than a Japanese fishing float. These small, renegade bubbles of glass, some of which escaped the woven nets of Japanese fishermen over a hundred years ago, have traveled across thousands of miles of open ocean. They have ridden the crests of tsunamis; they have been buffeted about by typhoons; they have escaped obliteration against the great steel hulls of cargo ships. And eventually, a few come to rest, battered but intact, on the rocky beaches of Oregon, Washington, and British Columbia.

In the summer of 2003, my husband and I celebrated our twentieth anniversary with a trip to Vancouver Island, a lush, idyllic blend of land and water, just a two-hour ferry ride from the cosmopolitan city of Vancouver. Exploring the island's small towns and coastal villages, it didn't take long for us to discover how thoroughly the inhabitants have embraced these sturdy, serendipitous gifts of glass that have washed up on their shores. Fishing floats were everywhere, in all sizes and colors, but mostly in endless shades of blue and green, as if they were born of the sea. We saw them lined up along windowsills, nestled in flowerbeds, and piled high in sandy baskets on the weathered front porches of beach houses. Yet they did not appear to be closely-guarded possessions. It was as though the hands that placed them there somehow understood and accepted that this was but another temporary stop in a long and restless journey.

Naturally, I found myself longing to find a fishing float of my own. This single-minded quest soon had me in full hunter-gatherer mode during our daily explorations of the remote beaches and coves that encircle the island. While I did gather indelible memories of fog-shrouded mornings giving way to brilliant breezy days, of misty evergreen forests pungent with the scent of cedar and pine, of salt spray and gray whales and puffins, I never did come upon a fishing float wedged among a scatter of driftwood or bobbing, jewellike, in a tide pool. Ultimately, I adopted a philosophical approach to my search, convincing myself to give it up to the universe, to happy chance, that with something like this, there was such a thing as trying too hard.

As it turned out, we spent the last day of our trip on another type of expedition—scouring the abundant local shops for gifts to bring home to family and friends. In particular, I needed to find something special for my mother, since by keeping our two children for ten days, she had made this whole trip possible. A well-traveled woman of discriminating tastes for whom T-shirts are decidedly not an option, Mom is not an easy person to buy for. It was one of those times when I had no idea what I was looking for; I only knew I'd know it when I found it. Unfortunately, it was growing late in the day and I hadn't found it yet. Time was running out when I came across a none-too-promising gallery perched on the second floor of a ramshackle clapboard building above a highly aromatic fishing charter outfit. Desperate, I climbed the crooked wooden staircase and was amazed to come upon a light-filled room brimming with original art and locally made crafts of every description. And there in the center of the room, suspended from the ceiling by varying lengths of fishing line and sparkling in the dusty sunlight, were a dozen or more fishing floats, girded by the artist with a narrow band of sterling silver and adorned on one side with a delicate silver starfish.

In the end, I bought four. One, of course, was for my feisty, elegant mother who was once told to give up her "girlish whim" of becoming a doctor, but became a fine one, anyway, and finished raising four children on her own when my father abruptly left after twenty-five years of marriage. One was for my sister and soul mate who nearly died of a brain tumor in 1999, but whose miraculous recovery and restored health is a constant source of joy and inspiration to everyone who knows her. The third was for a dear friend who had just lost her mother, but who somehow retained her infectious buoyancy despite a fickle undertow of grief. And the last one was simply an extra because I knew there would be another someday who would need such a beautiful talisman of resilience. Little did I know that less than three months later, it would turn out to be me.

It was not long after my diagnosis of early-stage breast cancer the following October that I unwrapped the remaining fishing float and hung it in my kitchen window. Facing east, it caught and held the first feeble light of many dark days that fall and winter. Through two surgeries and eight weeks of radiation, it offered both reminder and proof that I, too, could ride out the storm.

I still hope to find a fishing float "in the wild" someday, but until then, I've made up a story about being the first to find this one and it serves me well...

It is early morning on the far west coast of Vancouver Island. The fog has just lifted and I sit on a fallen log at that place where the dark, evergreen forest meets the sea. I'm alone on the wide, windswept beach with only the thundering surf and the cry of gulls for company. Shading my eyes with my hand, yet still squinting against the brightness, I scan the horizon, spotting here and there the distant, cloudlike sighs of the gray whales as they pass by on their way to the summer feeding grounds. Eventually, I lower my gaze to the shoreline, to the haphazard piles of driftwood and the tidal pools filling with the inrushing tide. All of a sudden, I see something unexpected amidst a tangle of kelp, and with a gasp of recognition, I leap up and run to the water's edge. I bend down to pick it up, pausing just long enough to rinse it in the waves. Standing in the wet sand, I cradle it with both hands, then laugh at myself for treating it so gently. I can see a tiny, hairline crack, can make out the shadowed pattern where the net used to be. I become aware of my own rapid breathing, of the sound of my pulse in my ears. I raise my arms, and lifting my treasure toward the racing clouds and climbing light, I marvel at how it has endured.

ACKNOWLEDGMENTS

I must first thank my dear friend and mentor, Maureen Ryan Griffin, without whose loving support and guidance this book would not exist. Over the years, her remarkable writing and creativity classes have transformed me from somebody who "always wanted to be a writer" into somebody who is one. I will be forever grateful for her wise counsel, her thoughtful and thorough editing, and for all the gentle and not-so-gentle nudging that helped me bring this dream into fruition.

An added benefit of Maureen's classes has been the fellowship with other Charlotte area writers, many of whom have become close friends. Special thanks to Emily Kern and Roxane Javid for their compassion, insight, and unrelenting encouragement as well as all the great heart-to-heart talks over coffee at Starbucks.

Other encouraging friends go a great deal further back and I would like to express love and appreciation to my best childhood buddy, Giuli Scanlon Doyle, who started supporting my writing dreams when we were in the fifth grade and hasn't stopped since, and to my college cohort and lifelong kindred spirit, Carol Shoun, whose abiding faith in God—and in me—has sustained me for more than forty years. Many thanks, also, to longtime friends Debbie Shutt and Carolyn Rosenblum for their steadfast support.

I am deeply grateful to my favorite high school English teacher, Mel Clark, who taught me how to read poetry—and how to love it—and who instilled a passion for Shakespeare that shows no sign of abating. His profound influence on my life continues through a now decades-long correspondence which allows us to exchange ideas about writing, books, music, and poetry of every kind.

To Mark Rumsey, news director at Charlotte's National Public Radio affiliate, WFAE 90.7 FM, my heartfelt gratitude for taking a chance on someone who, prior to 1998, had never seen the inside of a broadcasting booth, let alone spoken on the air. Through his expert coaching, I became a regular WFAE commentator and in the process, discovered a real love for this particular writing genre.

I must also acknowledge another friend and mentor, award-winning author Frye Gaillard whose willingness to assist aspiring writers is legendary throughout the Charlotte writing community and beyond. The combination of his writing talent, teaching skill, personal integrity, and wicked sense of humor is an ongoing source of inspiration.

And when it comes to inspiration, there is no greater wellspring than my cherished family. To the loving force of nature who is my mother, my thanks for never allowing me to doubt that I could do anything I set my mind to. To my father, my appreciation for a childhood full of summer trips and for the strong sense of place they engendered, not to mention all the priceless writing material. To my sister Claire, endless gratitude for her life-affirming spirit, her unquenchable sense of wonder, and her uncanny ability to read my mind. To my brother Fred, my thanks for his old-fashioned sense of honor as well as his ability to spin a yarn that will have me laughing until I cry. And humble thanks always to my late brother Rob, who, while not a writer, understood the importance of family stories and steered his life by the belief that a family is for keeps.

Finally, I want to thank my biggest cheerleaders, my husband Dana and our children, Mariclaire and Ian.

Mariclaire, thank you for your unquestioning belief in me and for all the ways you demonstrate it day by day. Working in secret on a website for the book and surprising me with it on Christmas morning was one of the nicest things anyone has ever done for me. Ian, thank you for the good common sense, wise-beyond-your-years insights, and quirky observations that fuel so many essays. You're a fun guy to have around. And Dana, thank you for the unconditional love and support that have helped me create the space to write. What a joy it is to document the everyday wonder of sharing this life with you.

My thanks to the editors in which these works first appeared:

"A Place by the Sea." First aired as a radio commentary on NPR affiliate WFAE 90.7 FM. Charlotte, NC. August 1999. Subsequently published in *The Charlotte Observer* 10 August 1999 (Copyright *The Charlotte Observer*—used with permission).

"A Taste for Lemon Sorbet." First aired as a radio commentary on NPR affiliate WFAE 90.7 FM. Charlotte, NC. January 2003. An abridged version later appeared in *Hungry for Home: Stories of Food from Across the Carolinas* by Amy Rogers. Charlotte, NC: Novello Festival Press, 2003. Also published in *On Air: Essays from Charlotte's NPR Station, WFAE 90.7*, edited by Scott Jagow, Marisa Rosenfeld, and M. Scott Douglass. Charlotte, NC: Main Street Rag Publishing Company, 2004, and *Spinning Words into Gold: A Hands-On Guide to the Craft of Writing* by Maureen Ryan Griffin. Charlotte, NC: Main Street Rag Publishing Company, 2006.

"Call It Like It Is." First aired as a radio commentary on NPR affiliate WFAE 90.7 FM. Charlotte, NC. November 2001.

"Deciphering the Zeroes." An abridged version aired as a commentary on NPR affiliate WFAE 90.7 FM. Charlotte, NC. July 1999.

"Don't Say." First appeared in *Kakalak 2006: An Anthology of Carolina Poets*, edited by Lisa Zerkle, Richard Allen Taylor, and Beth Cagle Burt. Charlotte, NC: Main Street Rag Publishing Company, 2006.

"False Spring." First appeared in *The Savannah Literary Journal 1998*. Savannah, GA: Savannah Writers' Workshop, Inc., 1997.

"It Goes Right Over our Heads." First aired as a radio commentary on NPR affiliate WFAE 90.7 FM. Charlotte, NC. May 2006.

"Lessons from the Night Sky." First aired as a radio commentary on NPR affiliate WFAE 90.7 FM. Charlotte, NC. October 2002. Subsequently appeared in *On Air: Essays from Charlotte's NPR Station, WFAE 90.7*, edited by Scott Jagow, Marisa Rosenfeld, and M. Scott Douglass. Charlotte, NC: Main Street Rag Publishing Company, 2004. Also appeared in *Spinning Words into Gold: A Hands-On Guide to the Craft of Writing* by Maureen Ryan Griffin. Charlotte, NC: Main Street Rag Publishing Company, 2006

"Let November Come First." An abridged version first aired as a radio commentary on NPR affiliate WFAE 90.7 FM. Charlotte, NC. November 1998. Subsequently appeared in *Today's Charlotte Woman: A Business/Lifestyle Magazine*, Holiday 1998. Later published in *Tis the Season: The Gift of*

Holiday Memories, edited by Tom Peacock. Charlotte, NC: Novello Festival Press, 2001.

"Make a Joyful Noise." An abridged version first appeared in *The Charlotte Observer* 01 December 2001 (Copyright *The Charlotte Observer*—used with permission).

"Maui Morning." First appeared in *Spinning Words into Gold: A Hands-On Guide to the Craft of Writing* by Maureen Ryan Griffin. Charlotte, NC: Main Street Rag Publishing Company, 2006.

"Out of My Hands." First appeared in *Spinning Words into Gold: A Hands-On Guide to the Craft of Writing* by Maureen Ryan Griffin. Charlotte, NC: Main Street Rag Publishing Company, 2006.

"Second Skin." First appeared in *The Charlotte Observer* 25 June 1996 (*Copyright The Charlotte Observer*—used with permission). Subsequently published in *A Second Chicken Soup for the Woman's Soul*, edited by Jack Canfield, Mark Victor Hansen, Jennifer Read Hawthorne and Marci Shimoff. Deerfield Beach, FL: Health Communications, Inc., 1998.

"Strong in the Ways of the Force." First aired as a radio commentary on NPR affiliate WFAE 90.7 FM. Charlotte, NC. May 2005.

"Stuffed." First aired as a radio commentary on NPR affiliate WFAE 90.7 FM. Charlotte, NC. November 2005.

"Teenspeak." First aired as a radio commentary on NPR affiliate WFAE 90.7 FM. Charlotte, NC. February 2005.

"The Power of Pie." First aired as a radio commentary on NPR affiliate WFAE 90.7 FM. Charlotte, NC. January 2005.

"Waltzing with Rhett." First appeared in *Skirt! Magazine*, June 2005.

ABOUT THE COVER ART

"An Invitation to Wonder" by Debbie Littledeer

I am grateful to one of my favorite North Carolina artists, Debbie Littledeer, for allowing me to use "An Invitation to Wonder" as the cover art for this book. In what was pure serendipity, I came across this image one rainy October afternoon while browsing through an arts and crafts gallery just off the Blue Ridge Parkway near Asheville.

A North Carolina native, Debbie Littledeer has lived in the Blue Ridge Mountains for most of her life and draws inspiration for her evocative and richly colored screen prints from the abundant natural beauty that surrounds her. She graduated from Mars Hill College in 1980 with a degree in Studio Art and Art History and has also studied at the Penland School of Crafts and the John C. Campbell Folk School. She has been screen-printing since 1986 and is a longtime member of the Southern Highland Craft Guild. Her work is sold in galleries and craft shops across the southeastern U.S. For more information, and to view a complete portfolio of available prints, please visit her website at: www.debbielittledeer.com.

49506643R00087

Made in the USA
Columbia, SC
24 January 2019